THE LONG HUNT

THE RYERSON PRESS TORONTO / WINNIPEG / VANCOUVER

THE LONG HUNT / FRED BRUEMMER

Printed and bound in Canada
by The Ryerson Press Toronto

SBN 7700 0264 1

Library of Congress Catalog Card Number 70-97222

To
Akpaleeapik
Akeeagok
Sam Willy
and Paulassee

with my thanks for taking me along

CHAPTER ONE

"Tea or coffee?"

The polite voice seemed to float into my sleep-drugged brain from far, far away. I became aware of the pervading drone of the great airplane and gradually groped back to reality. Patiently the pretty stewardess repeated: "Tea or coffee, sir?"

"Oh, coffee please," I mumbled mechanically, looking at my watch. Six A.M. We should be above Hudson Strait. I looked out of the window. Our plane was suspended in the greyness of a bleak morning.

Far below, ice and water formed an immense abstract painting, broad bands of black separating irregular masses of white. It looked cold, forbidding, unreal, like an artist's background in a painting of the Nordic Hel. I wondered briefly whether Henry Hudson had had some sort of premonition that this strait would lead him to death. It sure didn't look like the road to Cathay. In the plane it was hot and dry. My mouth felt parched, and the cookie I got with the coffee tasted like compressed sawdust.

The friendly but insistent voice of the stewardess was slowly bringing the other passengers back to life. They straightened out from the various contorted positions they had assumed to seek comfort and sleep, and slurped their coffee in morose silence. Still nattily dressed in now somewhat rumpled city suits, they hardly looked like people bound for the Arctic. They could have been a bunch of businessmen going to a convention. In fact they were the new men of the Arctic: teachers, technicians, electricians, engineers, administrators, clerks and mechanics and, possibly, the odd Mountie or missionary in mufti.

Startlingly out of place among this conservatively business-suited crowd were four slightly effeminate-looking pop singers, with long wavy hair flowing down to their shoulders and dressed in

1

cockerel-gay clothes. They were bound for Frobisher Bay on Baffin Island to entertain the natives at their annual spring festival. The white man's gift to the Eskimos, I thought a bit sourly.

The plane banked, landed smoothly and rolled down the long runway of Frobisher Bay to halt in front of the large Department of Transport hangar.

We climbed out, stiff after the six-hour flight, into a cold, grey day. The city-suiters rushed across the tarmac to the warmth of the DOT waiting room. I walked behind, feeling less conspicuous here in my arctic clothes than at Montreal's elegant Dorval airport, where everyone had looked at me as if I was some out-of-season Santa Claus. On the left, beyond the DOT buildings, I saw the familiar sprawling expanse of the Federal Building, an immense warren of corridors, rooms, halls, garages and offices, a mighty million-dollar memorial to cold-war futility. Once a United States Air Force base and, like so many others in the Canadian Arctic probably obsolete before it was finished, it had been turned over to the Canadian government. It was in this building that, on my first trip to the Canadian Arctic a few years earlier, I had been ruthlessly disabused of many romantic notions about the North, particularly the one that people go there because they like it, because of the space, the freedom, the romance of the North and all that sort of thing. The land of the men of the Last Frontier!

I went to have lunch in the Federal Building. A huge poster advised: TAKE AS MUCH AS YOU LIKE. EAT AS MUCH AS YOU TAKE. The food was excellent. I piled my tray, quite prepared to eat every last bit, as per instructions. A powerfully built man sat down at my table. I looked at him with reverence. Now finally, I thought, will I speak to one of those intrepid men of the North.

"How long have you been here?" I tried as an opening gambit.

"Four hundred and twenty-six days," he said, between mouthfuls.

"Oh, really?" I was taken aback by this unexpected preciseness.

"Yup. I've got a calendar in my room and I mark off the days I've been here. I've got two hundred and thirty-nine days to go."

"Then what?" I asked, a bit shocked. The look he gave me made me realize the question must have been exceedingly stupid.

"Then," he said with emphasis, "I get the hell out of here!"

"What's Apex Hill like?" I asked, trying to get onto a less sensitive subject.

"Don' know. Never been there!"

This really confused me. Apex Hill, only five miles away, is the "native" village where most of Frobisher Bay's Eskimos live.

"I guess you don't go out much?" I ventured.

"Nope, never do!" he agreed. "Why should I? There's nothing out there but snow and rock. All I need is here," and he made an expansive motion, as if to embrace the whole of the Federal Building. Since the place had given me, within a few hours, a bad case of claustrophobia, I shuddered at the thought of voluntary entombment within its walls.

Since my new friend was evidently not a man of the wide-open spaces, I asked, a bit meekly, why he had come north. He stared at me, amazed at so much naivety. Then he laughed.

"The money, man! The money! What do you think I came up here for? The climate?"

As I came to know the North better, I realized that my money-minded pioneer was neither the exception nor the rule. To some, the sole lure of the North is high wages. They regard their stay there as a form of well-paid exile. Others go because they like the comparative freedom a man can enjoy there and also, of course, because the pay is good. And some just go because they love the North. I think they are a minority but, unlike the others, they are a stable minority. The others serve their sentence, collect their sheckels (if they have not, out of sheer boredom, invested much of it already in liquor) and seek employment elsewhere. But those who love the North for itself—they stay, not always in the same settlement, but nevertheless always north. They all know each other, know all the tales and gossip from other settlements, because they all belong to one scattered community, linked by radio, voices that float through the ether across hundreds of miles of backyard. As one old-timer told me: "The Arctic is nothing but one big village with very wide streets!"

After the brief blast of fresh air, the DOT waiting room felt stiflingly hot. I looked around for familiar faces and stopped at the genially mephistophelian features of Bryan Pearson, long-time resident of Frobisher Bay, a free and often insolent spirit, and a persistent gadfly to stuffy officialdom. With his long hair, sunken cheeks, deep-set eyes and bristly pointed beard Bryan does look benevolently satanic and the Eskimos, in fact, refer to him fondly as "Satanassi." We once made a marvellous four-hundred-mile canoe trip together, all the way down Frobisher Bay to Kodlunarn Island, where Sir Martin Frobisher, nearly four hundred years ago, had dug up some two thousand tons of "gold ore." (Fool's gold, it turned out to be, and he got little thanks for his pains when he returned to England.)

Besides performing many more or less defined duties, Bryan acts as perennial impresario of Frobisher Bay's spring festival. He was at the airport to collect the long-haired pop quartet.

"Where are you going this time?" he asked.

"Grise Fiord," I said.

This seemed to confirm his often expressed opinion that I was slightly mad. He shrugged his shoulders. "Well, good luck! Say hello to Santa Claus!"

The Frobisher Bay passengers gradually disappeared in an assortment of government and private cars and taxis. Those bound for Resolute hung around the euphemistically named "Passenger Lounge" waiting for the Nordair plane to be readied for the last long leg of the flight north — with that traditional mixture of lassitude, ennui and impatience with which people await the departure of planes all over the world.

Finally the call came and the passengers trotted across the tarmac to the plane, hands cupped over freezing ears. The plane soared up and circled once above the settlement, already lilliputian below us — many-coloured toy houses in all shapes and sizes scattered, apparently at random, in the middle of nowhere. Our plane headed northwest across Baffin Island. Below, an infinity of snow, broken here and there by the gaunt dark ribs of rock ridges. Next stop, Resolute Bay and, with luck, on to Grise Fiord on Ellesmere Island, Canada's northernmost settlement.

I leaned back in my seat and tried to bring the events that led to this trip into some sort of focus. Arctic expeditions are supposed to require much organization, disciplined team work and a good supply of funds. In my case, the team work was negligible, since there was no team. Just me. The funds, unfortunately, were negligible too, consisting of my fairly slim savings. As to organization, that had been, at best, haphazard. Just as the idea for the trip had been haphazard.

Nine months ago I had flown with a Canadian Wildlife Service team across the Barren Grounds, counting caribou. That day it had taken us a long time to find the herd, south of Baker Lake. The sun was setting, and in its slanting rays the long line of migrating caribou had seemed like an endless yellow-coloured procession gliding across a dark earth. It was too late to do any counting. We flew high above the herd and marvelled at this yellow ribbon of life, strung out across the dark tundra, mile upon mile.

After we returned to Baker Lake, the only settlement in the Barrens, we ran across Hollis Shaw, maintenance supervisor and

4

man for all emergencies. Another one of that odd breed of men whom the North has ensnared. There are few settlements he does not know.

"Drop in for a drink," he said. After supper we trooped over. The talk turned to travel in the North. The days of the long solitary trips were past, we said. What a shame. Now an Eskimo hops on his skidoo, zooms off on a brisk hunting trip and is back in no time. Probably a lot more comfortable for him. But how unromantic!

"Well, there's one place at least where they still make some pretty long trips," Hollis said. "Gone for two, three weeks. Sometimes a month. Up in Grise Fiord. I know because I used to work there. They go after polar bears. Hunt them with dogs."

The talk drifted to other subjects, but I was no longer with it. My imagination was doing somersaults, shooting off in hyperboles of phantasy. To travel like that over the endless ice for weeks and weeks and weeks. How marvellous! "And how cold!" the little voice of reason tried to assert itself. And how are you going to get there in the first place? And if you do get there, do you think the Eskimos will be enchanted with the idea of lugging you along? And (most chilling) how are you going to pay for it?

Months later, I had broached the subject in Ottawa. I didn't say much about wanting to travel with the Eskimos. That sort of proposition, uttered in the orderly surroundings of a government office tends to sound absurd. I merely said I wanted to go to Grise Fiord to see and photograph the life of the people in this northernmost settlement of Canada. Having rather expected a blunt refusal of help of any kind, I was pleasantly surprised when we quickly reached an agreement suited to both the Department of Northern Development and me. In return for taking a considerable number of pictures specifically for the department, they would provide me with lodging and food in Grise Fiord for two months. The department would let me know when a plane under its charter would leave from Resolute for Grise Fiord and I would be able to ride on this plane, paying only standard passenger rate.

A quiet winter at home passed quickly. Then, one day in the middle of April, came the call from Ottawa. "Our plane is going to Grise Fiord on April nineteenth. If you catch the Nordair flight on the eighteenth, you can just make it."

Now I was on the way, wondering how things would turn out. Months earlier I had sent a message to Grise Fiord to say I was coming and that I wanted to accompany an Eskimo hunter on his spring trip. Would he take me? I was not looking forward to being stuck in the settlement for two months.

After five hours we reached Resolute, on Cornwallis Island: an airstrip and, near it, row upon row of long red-orange barracks, looking from on high like bricks neatly arranged in a vastness of white. This is the "Hub of the Arctic." Here large planes arrive from Montreal and Edmonton, and smaller planes take off to the remotest regions of the North. More than any place else on earth, the North is plane country. The children there may never have seen a tree, a chicken or a cow, and milk is something that grows in cans, but they can tell a Beaver from an Otter a mile away.

We stepped out into dazzling sunshine. Richard Bill, the area administrator was out there to meet me.

"Your plane for Grise Fiord leaves in half an hour," he said, pointing to a brilliantly painted twin-engine Otter. "Just time to grab a coffee." He shepherded me towards a building with the prominent and promising sign MUSKOX BAR. The bar was closed, but the coffee was good. There really was only time for a cup. The pilot was in a hurry.

"Weather forecast is bad," he explained.

We clambered into the plane, taxied out onto the runway—the propellers raising silvery eddies of snow—and took off, heading northeast. We crossed the broad, flat white sheet of Wellington Channel, the snow-covered mountains of western Devon Island and the contorted ice of Jones Sound. In the distance a dark, saw-edged line appeared. "Ellesmere Island," the pilot yelled into my ear. As we came closer, I could distinguish deep fiords cutting inland, flanked by brooding precipitous cliffs and, glittering blue-white in the distance, the ice caps and glaciers that lie on the land looking like an immense cleft-and-creased carapace. It was beautiful and at the same time grimly forbidding.

For the hundredth time the thought flashed through my mind: "How can anyone possibly exist here?" The pilot banked the plane and we swooped past the mighty cliffs, into a small bay and suddenly, incongruously, I could see a neat line of houses on a beach, some yellow, some red, square little boxes, overtowered by a soaring backdrop of deeply fluted cliffs. The plane banked again sharply and landed on a level stretch of ice, clearly marked by flags and barrels. The whole village, it seemed, awaited us, a mass of smiling brown faces, people laughing and jostling, all in peaked parkas. I jumped out and a tall man came forward. "I'm Roger Cousins. We've been expecting you. Welcome to Grise Fiord."

CHAPTER TWO

Grise Fiord is a new settlement. Its "natives," with the exception of the children, are not native to the place at all. They were brought to Ellesmere Island from Pond Inlet on northern Baffin Island and from Port Harrison, a settlement on the east coast of Hudson Bay. But while no Eskimos have lived in the last centuries on Ellesmere, Devon, Cornwallis and Bathurst Islands, they have in the past occupied most of Canada's northernmost islands, even to the very top of Ellesmere Island.

The Eskimos, or at least proto-Eskimos from whom the Eskimos eventually evolved, originated in Siberia and wandered, some five thousand years ago, to Alaska, across the landbridge that then linked the continents of Asia and America. From there they spread ever eastward, specks of humanity in the vastness of the arctic world. By about 2000 B.C. some of these first inhabitants of the Arctic had reached Ellesmere Island and travelled from there to Greenland. For the incredible span of nearly three thousand years, while far away Egyptian, Assyrian and Persian empires rose and crumbled, these people mastered the Arctic, their mode of life, attuned to this harsh environment, changing little in three millennia.

From Alaska to Greenland, they had one known trait in common. They fashioned exquisite tiny stone tools—burins, scrapers and microblades—out of chipped chert, flint or slate. Because of this, archaeologists call them the people of the Arctic Small Tool Tradition.

Their successors were the people of the Dorset Culture group, whose artifacts were first found near Cape Dorset on southern Baffin Island. Their culture probably evolved from that of the preceding group and they used many of the implements we now automatically associate with Eskimos: the crescent-shaped sealoil lamp, made of soapstone; the arctic sled, usually bone or ivory-shod; and possibly the kayak. They may also have invented that symbol of Eskimo life, beloved by cartoonists, the igloo. *Igloo* in Eskimo, by the way, does not mean snow-house. It just means house, any house, be it a sod hut, a prefabricated home or an administrator's substantial dwelling. Were an Eskimo to see Buckingham Palace he would, quite likely, refer to it as the Queen's igloo.

After holding sway over their arctic realm for nearly fifteen hundred years, the Dorset culture people were eased out or absorbed by waves of immigrants from the west, the men of the Thule culture. They began their gradual occupation of the Arctic about 900 A.D., and by 1100 A.D., they had reached Ellesmere Island and Greenland. Some rounded North-Greenland and migrated in slow stages down its east coast, others pursued sea mammals down Greenland's west coast until they came into frequently violent contact with the already established Viking settlers.

The Thule culture Eskimos owed their ascendancy at least in part to their ability to hunt and kill the great Greenland whale, called "bowhead" by the white men. Before European and American whalers hunted these whales to near-extinction they lolled in large pods near the edge of the ice, scooping up tiny crustaceans by the ton. The bowhead was a giant beast, up to sixty feet long, with a bulbous head and a mouth the size of a large living room. From the roof of the mouth about six hundred to eight hundred closely spaced baleen plates curved down, acting as a gigantic sieve to strain out the whale's minuscule prey. The whale was wrapped in a two- to three-foot-thick blanket of blubber weighing up to thirty tons, a marvellous floating oleaginous feast to any people fond of fat and able to catch it. The Thule Eskimos were experts at this feat and consequently could live in good-sized settlements, consisting of semi-subterranean houses with rafters made of whale bones, covered with hide and sod.

But then something went wrong. It may have been that during the Little Ice Age of the seventeenth and eighteenth centuries the whales no longer went as far north as they had been used to. Possibly depletion of whale stocks by European whalers had something to do with it. In any case the Thule Eskimos began a slow retreat from their northernmost reaches, and now only their stone and bone houses remain as reminders of their existence on the northernmost Canadian islands.

A single pocket of Eskimos remained in the far regions of the north. These were the Polar Eskimos of the Thule area in northwestern Greenland. For hundreds of years they lived alone, a tiny forgotten fragment of humanity so isolated they finally thought of themselves as being the only people on earth. One can imagine their surprise when, one bright day in 1818, two great sailing vessels squeezed their way through the ice and they were greeted by British naval officers in impeccable blue and gold. "Do you come from the moon?" asked the Eskimos.

Much of Ellesmere Island and the adjacent islands to the west was discovered and mapped by an extremely efficient Norwegian expedition under Otto Sverdrup in the years from 1898 to 1902. Later the Norwegians, with a good deal of justification, said this land was theirs by right of discovery. Canada was less than charmed to have a Norwegian annex in its arctic attic. After some haggling, the Norwegians, who were not all that keen to have this bit of far-away arctic real estate, abandoned their claim. To avoid repetition of such embarrassing claims, Canada rushed some expeditions of her own to the north, and topped this off by scattering Royal Canadian Mounted Police posts throughout the Arctic, scarlet-coated emblems of her sovereignty. Two posts were established on Ellesmere Island, on the east coast at Bache Peninsula and one at Craig Harbour on the south coast.

Since southern Ellesmere is a game-rich area, the Department of Northern Affairs decided to resettle it, and in 1953 the first Eskimo volunteers arrived. As a start they lived at Craig Harbour, but it didn't take them long to discover the white men had chosen the one place along the coast where the winds are worst. They decamped for mountain-sheltered Grise Fiord and, after shivering through a few more windswept winters, the Mounties followed.

When I arrived in Grise Fiord, its total population, Eskimo and white, numbered ninety-one. Strung out in a crescent on the level ground of a raised beach were the RCMP buildings, a small (and now nearly empty) Co-op store, the large, metal-roofed school with apartment annexes for the settlement's mechanic and teacher-administrator, and a long row of new, three-bedroom houses, supplied to the Eskimos by the government.

Two of the Eskimo men worked as special constables for the RCMP and another, Sam Willy, was the department's general factotum. He could repair anything, from a cantankerous motor to a seized-up sewing machine, hauled ice from a frozen-in iceberg, the village's only source of fresh water in winter, and carted away "honey bags," the euphemistically named plastic bags that line the strictly nonflush toilets in arctic settlements.

"The rest of the men are hunters," said Roger Cousins, the teacher-administrator, who had invited me for coffee the moment I arrived.

Grise Fiord on Ellesmere Island, Canada's northernmost settlement—Akpaleeapik lives in the first house of the front row

"Right now they are all away on the great spring hunt." He watched my face fall, then added, smiling, "Except two, Akpaleeapik and his brother Akeeagok, and they are among the best hunters. They may be willing to take you along. We'll see about that tomorrow."

It was late, when Roger brought me to "my" house, a sturdily built cabin with a sloping roof, on the next higher beach level and with a marvellous view over the settlement and the sound beyond— tranquil now in the roseate light of the sun's afterglow.

Pointing to the shelves stacked high with food, Roger said, "These are remnants of rations brought north by construction teams and survey crews. They ate what they liked, the rest they left. Just

10

Children play outside the Grise Fiord school during recess

11

help yourself. It's yours." After he left, I made a quick proprietary survey. Asparagus my predecessors had evidently not liked. There were seventy-five cans of it. As I made myself at home, everything still seemed rather unreal. Twenty-four hours ago I had been in Montreal. Now I was about as far north of it as Vancouver, on the Pacific, is to its west. And tomorrow I must arrange my trip with the Eskimos.

Akpaleeapik smiled and his broad strong face creased into a network of deeply etched lines. There was kindness in the face, but also an unmistakable shrewdness and I realized, uneasily, that at this moment he was probing tactfully to ascertain just how much of a nuisance I was going to be on the trip. Ruth, his daughter, who had spent many months in the south training to be a classroom assistant, and spoke good English, translated to the best of her ability the cautiously orchestrated overtures of both parties—mine careful and hopeful, Akpaleeapik's guardedly vague.

"Have you ever travelled by dogteam?" Akpaleeapik asked.

"Yes, in Foxe Basin. I spent some weeks with an Eskimo called Pewatook," I said, feeling like an applicant with slightly nebulous credentials.

Akpaleeapik pulled open a drawer and extracted a tattered copy of *Weekend Magazine.*

"Here are pictures of Pewatook," he said. "Ruth sent me the magazine when she was in the South."

"Those are my pictures," I said, trying to look modest, like a father whose child has just been praised by a passing stranger.

Now, I felt, was a good time to clinch the matter. We had already talked for an hour in Akpaleeapik's roomy kitchen, while his wife, Tataga, poured out cup after cup of tea. We had covered the subjects of weather, dogs, life in the North versus life in the South, children (mine and his), grandchildren (only his, thank heaven), skirting the real crux of the matter: how much would I pay and would he, at that price, take me along.

I took a deep drag on my cigarette and plunged.

Following pages:

Philapushee is Grise Fiord's oldest resident and only carver—when it is warm enough he sits on a small platform outside his house and, with simple tools, carves figures from soapstone

Annie, Philapushee's wife, keeps him company

Paulassee's children visited me often at my cabin—this little charmer brought her pet pup along

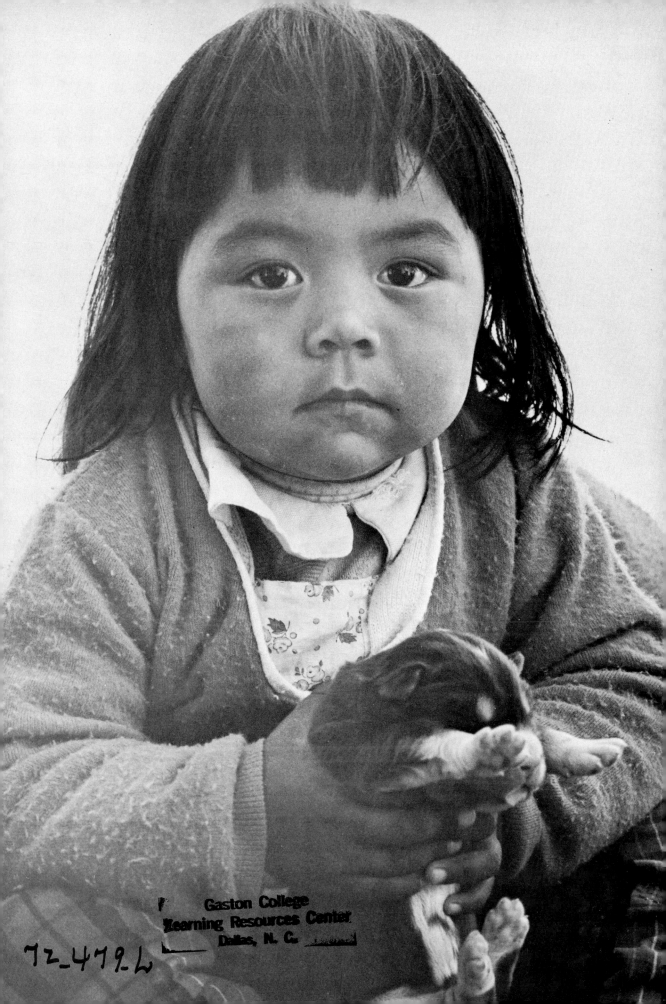

"Look, Akpaleeapik. I will pay you five dollars a day, for every day we travel together. I only want to come along. Where you go, and what you do, is your business. You're the boss. Also, we can take quite a bit of the food in the hut."

He considered this for a while, then looked straight at me. To be so blunt, I realized, had been a breach of etiquette. One should approach one's subject gradually and circuitously, not just burst out with it in this brusque fashion.

But Akpaleeapik was already inured to the white man's uncouth ways and he now, in turn, asked some straightforward questions.

"Will you travel at night?"

"Yes."

"What happens if you are cold?"

"I will run until I'm warm."

"Do you have enough clothes?"

"Yes."

"Maybe we go to Devon Island. Is that okay?"

"Yes, of course. I go where you go."

"Can you eat seal?"

"Yes. I've eaten it before and like it," I lied.

Akpaleeapik hesitated an instant. The next question was crucial.

"Will you travel on Sundays?"

"Sure. If you travel, I travel."

This is a touchy point, throughout the North. Many missionaries, imbued with a literal biblical fervour, had insisted that Sunday is a holy day. A day of rest. It might storm all week, with Sunday the only good day to hunt. That was just too bad. Home the hunter must stay and pray. The absurdity of foisting the mores of a pastoral Mediterranean people onto semi-nomadic hunters in the Arctic, never seems to have occurred to these missionaries. In most arctic settlements now, missionaries take a more realistic and tolerant view, but the Sunday work taboo still persists in some areas and Akpaleeapik was obviously worried about the prospect of having to spend every Sunday in the pit of an igloo just to please a prayer-prone passenger.

This hurdle passed, agreement was complete. We would first make a brief trip to northeastern Devon Island to hunt walrus and then embark on our long voyage in search of polar bear. The same afternoon, though, Akpaleeapik came to visit me and brought bad news. The first trip was off. He had just heard the government's X-ray team would fly in during the next days and neither he nor Akeeagok wanted to miss it.

Word of my obvious disappointment must have spread because in the evening I had another visitor, Sam Willy, looking now, in the harsh light of a single overhead bulb, spectrally gaunt, with his deep-set eyes and sunken cheeks. Despite his cadaverous looks, Sam is the kindest of men, ruggedly robust, and the father of a whole gaggle of round-cheeked girls.

After a lot of chitchat and pints of tea, Sam popped out with the real purpose of his visit.

"I go to Craig Harbour tomorrow," he said. "Maybe shoot walrus. You come?" Later I was to learn that he had dreamt up this trip just to cheer me up.

"You take food. I take gas. We go ten o'clock," Sam said. He was the owner of Grise Fiord's only skidoo, his pampered pride and joy.

CHAPTER THREE

It was a superb day to travel. A dark blue sky vaulted the scintillating white below; children in brightly coloured parkas tobogganed down a compacted snow slope on their bottoms, and out on the ice the tethered huskies joined in a chorus of happy howls. Sam had already packed the sled, wider and shorter than most dog sleds, and hitched it with a long thong to the rear of the skidoo. Near the front of the sled he had put the food box and lashed a couple of caribou skins over it, to give me a comfortable, though somewhat precarious perch.

Sam, half kneeling, half crouching on the elongated saddle of his beloved machine, eased the skidoo cautiously through the maze of upthrust ice blocks in the tidal area along shore. On the level ice beyond he opened the throttle wide, and we zipped along, the sled slewing alarmingly.

After two hours we stopped at the scene of a strange battlefield. Frozen guts trailed through the snow, like a mass of bleached, convoluted sausages. Streaks and puddles of blood, discoloured to a pale pink, were frozen into snow and ice. Half a dozen partially caved-in igloos stood in a semicircle.

"*Savssat*," Sam said.

We made tea in one of the abandoned igloos. Last fall, Sam explained, about one hundred and fifty belugas, or white whales, became trapped in this bay by a sudden freeze-up. Since they must surface every fifteen minutes or so to breathe, they could not swim the long distance under the new ice to open water beyond without suffocating. To survive, the animals had to keep a breathing hole open in the encroaching ice. This hole of a trapped whale pod is called *savssat* by the Eskimos.

Narwhal, the long-tusked unicorns of the Arctic Sea, also get trapped occasionally in a bay or fiord when fast-forming ice covers

18

its entrance. Peter Freuchen, the veteran arctic traveller, reported, "We have seen 1,000 animals trapped this way . . . one can hear the noise the unfortunate animals make miles away." Porsild, a Danish scientist, wrote a monograph on a particularly large narwhal savssat on the northwest Greenland coast. The massed tusks of the narwhal surfacing in this constricted place, looked, he said, from a distance like *chevaux de frise.*

The trapped white whales were in a desperate situation. Each moisture-laden breath they exhaled into the subzero air settled as ice on their prison's rim. At first the savssat had been large, more than fifty yards across. But each day the icy rim crept closer inwards until, to breathe, the frantic animals had to jostle up in a tight mass.

An Eskimo, returning from a hunting trip, discovered the savssat. During the dark winter months, when the moon was full, the Eskimos travelled out to the hole to kill whales for themselves and their dogs. The dark whale meat tastes good, but what the Eskimos really like is *muktuk,* the thick rubbery skin of the whales. It tastes rather like hazelnuts and is extremely rich in vitamin C.

At temperatures of forty and fifty below, in the pale blue light of the moon, the Eskimos harpooned close to a hundred of the glistening white whales, shot them and dragged them out onto the ice. Sled-load after sled-load of meat, blubber and skin was hauled back to Grise Fiord. And while the dead whales were being heaved out of the hole, the survivors kept bobbing up in the dark pool of water and blood, to breathe the life-giving air.

No one expected them to survive but, having taken enough to give the people and dogs in Grise Fiord an ample supply of food until spring, the Eskimos left the last fifty whales in peace. Slowly, inexorably, the ice closed in on them. Their gelid exhalations began to freeze into an ice-cupola that domed over their hole. The whales apparently lived mainly off their blubber. The stomachs of those killed by the Eskimos were empty, and some had only a thin blubber layer left. But all during the long, dark winter they kept pushing up towards air in that constricted hole in a frightful frantic jostle. Then, one day in March, they were gone. A tide crack must have opened up, and along this fissure the last surviving, emaciated whales swam out to open water. There is a large "polynia," as these open-water areas in the Arctic are called (they never freeze over, no matter how cold it gets), in the vicinity of Cobourg Island, near the entrance to Jones Sound. This is a favourite wintering area of sea mammals, and to it the near-doomed whales escaped.

Now a ringed seal had taken over the abandoned savssat. These seal remain in the Arctic all year. When the sea freezes over, they nibble several holes into the ice. As the ice thickens to five and six feet, the seals keep chomping away to keep their breathing holes open, vital vents to the air above.

After we had reloaded the sled, Sam took his rifle. We walked together to the seal's breathing hole.

"Now walk away, loudly, and wait at that igloo," Sam whispered.

I stomped off towards the igloo. Sam remained stooped over the hole, hoping the seal would interpret the retreating steps as an all-safe signal, and come up in this hole to breathe. I had hardly reached the igloo, when the gun went off and a geyser of blood and water spattered up from the hole. Sam dropped the gun and grabbed the seal, its head smashed by the heavy bullet. I got a thong from the sled, Sam slipped it in through one eye socket and out the other and we hauled the seal out onto the ice.

"We'll pick it up on the way back," Sam said. He started the skidoo and off we went.

Near King Edward VII Point, jutting far out into Jones Sound, a glittering procession of sharp-ridged icebergs soared skyward like blue-white spires. They regularly drift across Baffin Bay from the

Having shot a ringed seal in its breathing hole, Sam Willy hauls the animal out of the water

glaciers of Greenland. Since the summers are short and fairly frigid, and they spend most of the year trapped in ice, large bergs may last a decade before they melt and disintegrate. Some of these, into which wind and water had worn smooth oval holes, looked like giant Henry Moore sculptures.

The major portion of an iceberg is below water and, even in winter (trapped in six-foot ice), it is slowly shifted by tides and currents and surrounded by a wide circle of wildly upthrust ice blocks. There are rifts and clefts near the berg, where water wells up, and here walrus haul out to sleep on the ice.

Unlike the ringed seal, the walrus is unable to chomp a breathing hole through the ice. It must either stay at the edge of open water or find wide "leads" of open water zigzagging through the ice, or holes near icebergs. When not diving for mussels and clams (their main food, which they rake up from the sea bottom with their curved ivory tusks), walrus like to hoist their mighty bulk onto an ice pan, or firm ice, near a lead and sleep. Sometimes they sleep too long. Tides and currents, which rip the ice sheet apart to form leads, may also snap them shut. Then the locked-out walrus must hump laboriously over ice and snow in search of another lead or an area of open water. Nearly every spring Grise Fiord hunters encounter on their long trips such wandering walrus, dragging their one-ton bulk along, desperately seeking open water. Sometimes both their enormous strength and their fat reserves give out. Sam Willy found a dead and completely emaciated walrus on Jones Sound some years ago.

We drove to each berg, stopped the skidoo some distance away

In the greyish gloom of a whiteout, Sam Willy fills the tank of his skidoo near some old igloos, built by white whale hunters months earlier

and walked up to it, Sam with his rifle at the ready. Near some icebergs we saw the telltale dark brown smudge where walrus had snoozed on ice; but all of them were now safely in the water. Maybe it was too cold. It was twenty below and the icy wind was cutting through our heavy clothes. Sam pumped up the pressure stove in the lee of an iceberg, we drank some scalding hot tea, felt less shivery, then headed for Craig Harbour, stopping briefly near a small island where Sverdrup, stuck for an unexpected fourth winter in the Arctic, had built a large cairn and left a record of the expedition in a metal cylinder.

"Breast Island," Sam explained, as we looked for the cairn. On the white man's maps it is coyly called Cone Island.

Eskimo names tend to be descriptive: Muskox Mountain, Crouching-Dog Butte, Kidney Lake. Many appellations, though, draw heavily for similes on the more private parts of the human anatomy. The early whalers, too, liked evocative names such as "The Maiden's Paps," for a pair of prominent peaks. This earthy nomenclature of Eskimos and whalers has been barred from maps, with such bland but safe names as King Edward Point serving as substitute.

We did find several cairns, half buried in snow, but I knew the records had long been removed and we scrambled down to reach Craig Harbour before night. A barrier of ice blocks barred the mouth of the bay and it took all of Sam's skill to manoeuvre the skidoo through this frigid maze. It wasn't until we reached smooth ice near the head of the bay that I saw the old RCMP house, white, with shingled roof and gables, all alone on a raised beach. Beyond, a wide valley curved up into the mountains.

There were beds in the house, a table and chairs, a large stove and a shelfful of emergency rations. We found some coal in a bin behind the house and soon had a good fire crackling in the stove. I cautiously thawed out the cameras. The Rolleiflex had worked fine, but when I opened the Nikon, film chips fell out like confetti. The film had become brittle in the cold and the wheel teeth of the advance had ripped through the sprockets. From then on I carried this camera under my parka and a couple of spare rolls of film in my pockets.

"You've frozen your face," said Sam reproachfully.

I looked in the piece of mirror on a shelf. Where my chin and cheek had touched the parka zipper, when I snuggled into it to escape the wind, red welts were raised in parallel lines. Later they turned dark brown, dried and peeled.

Near Cone Island we passed some weirdly sculpted icebergs with great oval holes

Early next morning we walked up the valley, grooved by a deep river-bed in its centre. It had been bitterly cold that night and frost haze hung like a bluish veil over the valley. The wind had died down and a breathless frozen hush lay on the land, broken only by the squeak of our boots on the hard snow.

Sam had hoped to show me muskoxen, but we only found a bleached skeleton, the massive horns curving out of the snow. We were looking at it, when a long-drawn, mournful howl broke the stillness and reverberated from the valley walls; a call lonely and wild, and strangely in harmony with this rugged and lonely land. Once more the wolf howled, then there was again utter silence.

Sam scanned the valley with his binoculars. To me, the wolf was a beautiful free animal. Ever since I had had the good fortune to observe the great white arctic wolves closely during a summer spent on the Barren Grounds, I had felt an admiration for these powerful solitary predators. (Unlike the timber wolf of more southern regions, the arctic wolf, who can weigh up to one hundred and fifty pounds, does not hunt in packs). To Sam, the hunter, the wolf was eighty dollars, forty for bounty and forty for the pelt. But, despite a long careful search, he failed to spot the animal.

We walked up the valley, found no trace of muskoxen, returned to wrench the great skull loose from the skeleton, then slithered down the hard snow to the river-bed below. There we found the wolf's tracks. We had looked everywhere, except down. The wolf had been thirty yards away, screened by the river bank, while we scanned the valley walls for miles around.

We drove back to Grise Fiord along the coast of Ellesmere Island, stopping briefly below the sheer, greenish wall of Jakeman Glacier, a coruscating cascade of ice, creased, crevassed and criss-crossed by deep blue veins. Fram Fiord nearby, had been named by Sverdrup for his ship, the famous *Fram.* Fridtjof Nansen had designed this ship and the Scot Colin Archer had built her with such a rounded bottom that, taken in the frightful nip of the arctic ice, she would pop up rather than be crushed. After Nansen had made his famous expedition through the polar ice in the *Fram*, with Sverdrup as her captain, the stout vessel had been refitted and headed again for the Arctic, this time with Sverdrup in the dual role of expedition leader and captain. A storm sprang up when he reached Cone Island, and he had found refuge in the deep narrow Fram Fiord. It was summer then and the valley beyond the fiord was verdant. "We trod on grass or sank into a soft carpet of moss . . . [and] hares were hopping about in the dusk,"[1] Sverdrup wrote.

[1] From Otto Sverdrup, New Land, translated by Ethel Harriet Hearn, 2 vols. (London: Longmans, Green & Company, 1904).

Craig Harbour was an RCMP post from 1922 to 1956—now the house stands abandoned, but it is still in good shape. Sam Willy looks for muskoxen.

Now the valley was icy, but there were still hares—large arctic hares, with snow-white downy fur and black ear tips. About a dozen of them were nibbling the sparse, sere blades of grass on a boulder-strewn bench above the frozen river, standing straight up occasionally on their hind legs, like white-robed, longeared little men; they regarded us with more curiosity than fear, and I felt deeply sorry for the trusting animals. But Sam, who after all hunts to eat and would in any case have regarded any such scruples as ludicrous, quickly shot five of them. The others scattered in panic. He eviscerated the animals, and we lugged the now blood-smeared corpses back to the sled.

At the savssat we stopped again, loaded the killed seal on the back of the sled and headed for home in a chill bluish dusk. Throughout the trip the sled had shown a nerve-wracking tendency to slew, whenever Sam speeded up. Most of the day we had crept cautiously through the tortuous ice along the coast. Now we had a long level stretch before us, twenty miles of smooth snow or dark, wind-polished ice. Sam opened the throttle wide, crouched low behind his windshield, quite unaware that behind him his passenger was in bad trouble.

A wind-and-water-sculpted iceberg serves Sam Willy as lookout while he searches Jones Sound for signs of polar bear

Sam Willy eviscerates arctic hares he has shot in Fram Fiord

With the weight of the seal and the hares on the back, the sled now veered wildly, careening from side to side in ever-widening arcs, while I clung to the lashing ropes as desperately as a baby monkey to its leaping mother. I screamed and screeched and hollered but, deafened by the roar of his machine, Sam drove blithely on. Then the inevitable happened. With the full force of an outward swing, one of the runners struck a small ice hummock. The sled tilted and lurched and I was catapulted off, landing on the ice with a bang that knocked the breath right out of me. I slithered on my back across the polished ice, huddling my camera bag, to fetch up with a resounding crack against an ice block. It knocked me out. When I came to, groggy and sick to my stomach, Sam, skidoo and sled were dark dots in the distance. I got up and began to follow them, a strange throbbing noise in my ears. After what seemed a very long time, I could see the skidoo turn and come racing back.

By the time it arrived, I felt better and inclined to laugh the whole thing off as another of those experiences that are amusing provided you are not seriously hurt. But Sam was terribly upset. He asked at least twenty times, "Are you really okay?"; insisted I sit down while he repacked the sled and treated me with the guilty solicitude one would be apt to show a pregnant woman whom one had accidentally knocked down a flight of steps. It was again vividly impressed on me, how very responsible Eskimos feel for the *kabloona* (white man) who travels with them. Not quite without reason, they regard him as an accident-prone nincompoop and look after him like a father taking his five-year-old son tobogganing on a rather steep slope. Quite possibly, bringing back a severely damaged kabloona, though it happened through no fault of his, may mean loss of face to an Eskimo. In any case, Sam drove the rest of the way to Grise Fiord as if he had a crate of raw eggs on his sled and we arrived late at night. On the ice of the bay squatted the chartered DC-3 that had brought the X-ray team. We had returned in time for Sam's chest to be probed by Roentgen's invisible rays.

28

CHAPTER FOUR

The next days passed quickly. I drifted from house to house, photographing the daily domestic life of the Grise Fiord Eskimos. The houses were spotless. Boots were left outside and everyone walked around in socks or duffel slippers. There were refrigerators in many kitchens and washing machines in nearly all. Most families had record players or tape recorders—Western music and Scottish reels were favourites.

Roger's wife, Mary (herself an Eskimo from Pond Inlet where her father, Kayak, has been special constable of the RCMP for more than thirty years), had worked unstintingly at helping the Grise Fiord women to master the art of housekeeping—solving such problems as how to make a cake with a cake mix, when you can't read the instructions. Mary has lived for years in the South and has travelled widely in Europe and Africa. She brought to this task not only the Southerner's *savoir-faire* with gadgetry, but a shrewd appreciation of which of the white man's goods are mere gaudy trash, and which ones could be genuinely useful to her people. In this way she had helped to ease the transition from igloo and tent, to hut, to large comfortable house—not with the benevolent condescension of so many whites who wish to transform the "primitive" people of the North to their image, but with the intuitive understanding of a highly educated Eskimo for her own people.

People like Mary who can, to some extent, fuse the material and ethical values of such disparate cultures as that of the white man and the Eskimo into a new and fairly harmonious concept of life are, unfortunately, rare in the Arctic. In many settlements the over-whelming impact of the white man's culture has all but wiped out the Eskimo culture. There it becomes tragically true what the famous Austrian ethologist Konrad Lorenz said about the super-imposition of cultures, in his book *On Agression*:[1] "... it is usually

[1]Konrad Lorenz, *On Aggression* (New York: Harcourt, Brace & World, 1966).

29

highly dangerous to mix cultures. To kill a culture, it is often sufficient to bring it into contact with another, particularly if the latter is higher, or is at least regarded as higher, as the culture of a conquering nation usually is. The people of the subdued side then tend to look down upon everything they previously held sacred and ape the customs which they regard as superior. As the system of social norms and rites characteristic of a culture is always adapted, in many particular ways, to the special conditions of its environment, this unquestioning acceptance of foreign customs almost invariably leads to maladaptation . . . [they find it easiest] to imitate the most superficial, least valuable customs of the other."

The British historian Arnold J. Toynbee in *A Study of History*[1] terms the Eskimos people with an "arrested civilization." They achieved the tour de force of living in an arctic environment "and adapted their life to its exigencies with consummate skill." In so doing, they reached an ultimate of specialization and had to pay the penalty of a "rigid conformation of their lives to the annual cycle of arctic climate." With the material means at their disposal, they could hardly advance any further, and their civilization had become static.

It was obviously necessary and desirable to change the Eskimo's mode of existence. Ideally, in this transformation, the best elements of his culture would have been retained and fused with the most suitable concepts of Western life. This would have required teachers and administrators imbued with understanding, knowledge and tact. Some, like Roger and Mary Cousins, have these qualities. To others, the Eskimos were simply rather primitive "natives" who had to be somehow elevated to white man's stature.

And on the subject of "natives," Toynbee offers a chilling reflection: "When we Westerners call people natives, we implicitly take the cultural colour out of our perception of them. We see them as wild animals infesting the country in which we happen to come across them, as part of the local flora and fauna and not as men of like passions with ourselves. So long as we think of them as 'natives' we may exterminate them or, as is more likely today, domesticate them and honestly (perhaps not altogether mistakenly) believe that we are improving the breed, but we do not begin to understand them."

It is this lack of understanding which, so frequently, hampers harmonious co-operation in the North. The Eskimos, since they have little choice, will acquiesce to dictates emanating from some authority far away in the south, where men of good will and high

---

[1] Arnold J. Toynbee, *A Study of History* (London and Toronto: Oxford University Press, 1935-1961).

idealism concoct marvellous plans and send them like panaceas to the north and can't understand why the Eskimos, who have never been consulted, fail to hail it all with shouts of glee. In settlements like Grise Fiord, where many problems are settled by an elected Eskimo council, with the administrator acting as advisor, decisions are reached in a way both acceptable and understandable to the people of the community, and such decisions then have their support. It is to be hoped that in the years to come, the white man's rule by fiat, however high-principled and well-meant, will give way to a mode of government in which the Eskimos will have a measure of control over their own culture and destiny.

While I was taking pictures and spending long, interesting evenings at the hospitable home of Roger and Mary, Akpaleeapik and Akeeagok were busy preparing for the trip. Traces were checked, dog harnesses repaired, weapons cleaned and oiled, and tools carefully packed. One evening Akpaleeapik came to my house with a coffin-sized wickerwork hamper and we selected food from the shelves, mainly bulk fare: bags of rice, noodles, sugar and large cans of suety bully beef which my predecessors had evidently disdained. The hunters' wives made new *kamiks* (sealskin boots) and repaired old ones, and checked and repaired their men's entire travelling wardrobe. Tataga made me a pair of kamiks, the soles of strong bearded seal leather, the shafts of ringed seal, with alternating bands of light and dark fur to make an attractive pattern.

Since the zipper of my down parka had burnt my face so badly on the first trip, Roger lent me a zipperless, two-layer Eskimo style parka—the inside duffel, the outside a strong white twill (the hood framed with wolverine fur), and voluminous enough to carry one or two cameras underneath. This made me look distinctly pregnant and it became a standard joke throughout the trip for either Akeeagok or Akpaleeapik to tap me on the tummy and ask: "How many months?"

We left Grise Fiord on April 28. It was a marvellous day, clear and cold and windless. By the time all the boxes, the great hamper, the sacks with spare thong, harnesses and sleeping bags had been piled onto our sled, covered with several layers of caribou skins and a large polar bear skin, the twenty-six-foot sled carried a seven- or eight-hundred-pound load. Akpaleeapik's sled was new, the broad low runners shod with iron, and the transverse pieces lashed to them with nylon rope. The fifteen dogs were harnessed, yelping and squirming with eager excitement. Nearly everyone in Grise Fiord had come to see us off. We shook hands all around, slipped on goggles and mittens, hopped on the sled, Akpaleeapik in front, his eldest son, Iseechee, in the centre and I, high on the hamper, in the rear. Our departure was abrupt and undignified. The Eskimos who had held the over-eager dogs leapt back, the huskies hurled themselves forward, galloping faster and faster as the heavy sled gained momentum and we caromed in a crazy zigzag course through the jumble of ice blocks in the tidal zone, the sled swaying and tilting, with me clinging to the lashings like a limpet, horrified by the idea of being pitched off again, this time in front of the assembled community.

After a mile or so, the dogs stopped their enthusiastic gallop and settled down to a steady trot. Our team consisted of fourteen huskies of assorted sizes and colours, ranging from black to buff to cream and white, and mixtures of all of these colours, and one big black Labrador retriever, named Apapak.

Actually only Apapak's father was a true Labrador (he had belonged to Roger); his mother was a husky, but he had taken nearly entirely after his father. Big, eager, willing but clumsy, Apapak was the original underdog, always traipsing into trouble. If there was a hidden fissure in the ice, Apapak was sure to fall into it. If an ice block barred the way, all the huskies would pass it on the right, while Apapak blithely and apparently absentmindedly headed left,

Travelling along the south coast of Ellesmere Island

only to be rudely yanked back as his trace snagged around the base of the block. The huskies, while harbouring towards each other a long list of hierarchical grudges, were unanimous only in their contempt and hatred for Apapak. Given the slightest provocation, or none at all, they would suddenly fling themselves on the poor mutt, their vicious yelps and snarls topped by the shrill, frightened falsetto trill of Apapak.

This was another of his unfortunate peculiarities. Huskies howl and other dogs bark, but Apapak could do neither. The best thing he could produce from that massive chest of his was a sort of canine coloratura, and the more frightened he was the higher rose his pitch, until it sounded like a hundred off-key canaries. Another of Apapak's problems was, that as a pup, he had been the family's pet. Now a hefty hundred pounder, he still thought of himself in that role, always friendly and affable, seeking and expecting nothing but love. Among that pack of snarly huskies, poor Apapak was like a sheep amongst a fold of wolves. Although he was bigger than all the huskies and probably stronger than most, he was frightened witless by them. Let the smallest husky bare his fangs, and Apapak would instantly and abjectly throw himself on his back, and screech in treble tremolo.

We travelled fast over smooth ice past the mouth of Grise Fiord and stopped briefly at the next headland where Akpaleeapik checked his fox traps. He returned after a while with two foxes, frozen solid in the contortions of death. While he made tea, the second sled, with Akeeagok and his oldest son Seeglook, caught up with us. Both boys should really have been in school, but the fathers had asked Roger to allow them to come along. It seemed important that, in addition to school learning, the boys should acquire the art of travelling and hunting in the Arctic, and with this concept Roger, unlike many teachers in the North, agreed.

The cousins were as different as their fathers. Akpaleeapik, forty-five years old, had come to Ellesmere Island from the Pond Inlet area of Baffin Island. He was a powerfully built man, compact and muscular. His sometimes severe authoritarianism was tempered by kindness. He was the sort of man who automatically assumes command and whom other men, equally automatically, obey. Akeeagok, eight years younger, was devoted to his brother. His admiration for Akpaleeapik knew no bounds. "He has taught me everything I know about hunting," he would often say. Unlike the stern Akpaleeapik, Akeeagok was a gay spirit, happy, hardworking and incredibly tough.

Iseechee, eleven years old, tall for his age and gangly, loved and admired his father immensely, but also stood in awe of him. This made him both eager and insecure, and since he was a natural-born stumblebum, he tripped into trouble with devastating regularity. Sometimes it was pathetic to see how his eagerness to please his father, clashed with his sense of insecurity. Once our tents were up, Akpaleeapik looked after the dogs, I got supper ready, and Iseechee had to light the pressure stoves, fetch fresh-water ice and put everything inside the tent in its appointed place.

While I was opening cans or cutting up meat, Iseechee would kneel next to me in an agony of indecision. One could see the questions tumble through his mind: "Should I get ice first? But then father will come and the Primus stove is not filled! Maybe I should do that first. Ah, damn it, the kabloona is nearly ready and he will need the Coleman stove to cook supper! Maybe I should fill the Coleman stove first! But the boxes are not yet in place, maybe father wants that first!" Thus he would dawdle and fidget, start to do this and abandon it, getting more and more flustered as the sounds from outside indicated that the dogs were fed and his father would return any moment.

Then, in a sudden outburst of worried energy, he would try and do all things at once, with absolutely catastrophic results, and in the midst of chaos Akpaleeapik slipped into the tent and poor Iseechee caught hell. Despite these daily woes, he enjoyed the trip, and on the rare occasion when he had done everything right and his father mumbled a grudging word of approval, Iseechee's worried face would flush with pleasure. At such times he was deeply happy.

Seeglook, a year older than Iseechee, was a miniature edition of his cheerful, happy-go-lucky father, a round and rosy-cheeked bundle of energy, always up to some mischief, the sort of boy who can't see a steep snow slope without clambering up and slithering down. He and his father were pals, and at night we could hear them talk and laugh from the neighbouring tent.

To both boys the trip, with all its periodic hardships, was a marvellous lark and adventure and they dreampt up a hundred games en route to enliven the sometime tedious travel over monot-onous stretches of snow and ice, when all of us began to nod

Facing page:

The boys guard the dogs while their fathers check fox traps near the base of towering cliffs on Ellesmere Island

sleepily to the rhythm of the gently pitching sled. Then Seeglook would hop off, race over, sneak up behind Iseechee and, with one push, send him sprawling into the snow. Or Iseechee, warned by the stealthy crunch-crunch-crunch of boots in the brittle snow, pretended to sleep soundly and at the last instant, turned and tripped the running Seeglook.

The boys' main job was to look after the dogs when their fathers were away checking traps, looking for polar bears or stalking seal, and to untangle the traces. The dogs were hitched fan-shape, each with his own trace, ranging in length from twenty-five to thirty-five feet. Throughout the day, the dogs shuttled endlessly from left to right and right to left, hopping over or ducking under the other dogs' traces, plaiting them gradually into one thick braid. When we stopped, the boys had to unravel this tangled skein. It looks like an utterly hopeless task, but the traces, made of bearded seal leather, are too stiff to pull into tight knots, yet supple enough to be easily handled. One by one the boys extricated each trace from the braid, and reattached the far ends to the dogs, slipping the terminal loops over the toggles on the dogs' harnesses.

We sledged until 8 P.M., past Harbour Fiord, where the *Fram* had passed the second winter while Sverdrup and his men explored "new land" (this is the title of the book he later wrote) to the west and north, to the soaring cliffs of South Cape. Here we set up our first camp.

Our tent was ten feet long, seven feet wide with a single ridgepole supported by two end-poles, and held taut by a ring of long guy ropes. Akeeagok's tent was somewhat smaller. The moment the tent was up, Akpaleeapik crawled in and Iseechee and I handed him, through the flap, the rolled-up skins: first the large polar bear skin laid on the snow, hair down, and then the caribou skins on top, fur side up. The bottom flaps of the tent were weighed down with sacks full of clothing, dog food, spare harnesses and traces, and with boxes containing tools, pressure stoves, dishes and cutlery. Everything in the tent had its exact place, and the sequence in which pelts, sacks and boxes were passed into the tent, and their arrangement inside, never varied.

The cameras I left in a box on the sled, since they would only steam up in the tent, and the film, too, was left outside to avoid the

Facing page:

In the evening we stop near South Cape and prepare to set up camp under a flaring sun

danger of moisture condensation on the frigid film surface. When I wanted to take pictures inside, I would slip the Nikon under all my clothes and carry it there, like an icy incubus, until it had warmed up sufficiently not to become covered with moisture in the humid atmosphere of the tent.

By common consent I was elected cook of the expedition. The first evening Akpaleeapik said: "You cook!" and cook I was for the next six weeks. This placed no strain on my culinary abilities. After a long day of travel, we were invariably famished. Whatever I concocted was eagerly eaten, and even such slips as throwing, absentmindedly, a handful of tea leaves into the breakfast porridge raised scant comment. As long as I cooked white man's fare, however ghastly, my Eskimos ate it, if not with gusto, at least without criticism; but once we started on venison, they did try to teach me the rudiments of Eskimo cuisine: polar bear and caribou *without* salt, and seal *with* salt—and looked distinctly pained when I got this mixed up.

Lovely but doomed: a little arctic fox taken in Akpaleeapik's trap

After supper we walked through the maze of ice blocks to the coast to check traps, set on a raised, windswept beach, where snow was not likely to bury them. We found a dead fox in one trap and then a live one in another—looking at us, half resigned and half terrified, with brilliant amber eyes, its mangled front foot held in the steel jaws of the trap. Akpaleeapik stepped on the fox, crushing its rib cage, and the animal died with a mournful mewing sigh.

Back in the tent, Akpaleeapik immediately began to skin the still-warm fox with a small penknife: he first freed the paws and pulled the legs out of the skin, loosened the tail from its bone, then pulled the fox out of his skin as one pulls a hand out of a glove, and threw the tiny emaciated cadaver out of the tent. We brewed another pot of tea, our fifth or sixth that day, spread our sleeping bags on the fur platform, built up pillows with rolled-up parkas and sledging pants and crawled into our sacks, Akpaleeapik on one side, I on the other, and Iseechee in the centre.

An empty quart can stood in each reach, as our communal chamber pot, a very essential item, since we daily drank tea by the gallon. Akpaleeapik, with the easy skill of long practice, could use the can without leaving his sleeping bag. Iseechee and I, less assured, crawled shiveringly out of our warm bags, used the can and poured the contents into the snow, at the head of our bed, where the warm liquid disappeared instantly, leaving a small yellowish hole—a neat and odourless disposal.

Getting up was a delightfully drawn-out process. At this latitude and time of year the sun scarcely dipped below the horizon at night, and later during the trip the nights were nearly as bright as the days, so it mattered little whether we travelled day or night. We no longer lived on a twenty-four-hour rhythm, but on one dictated by the exigencies of travel and hunting. "Night" was when we went to bed, be it 8 P.M. or 8 A.M., and morning came ten to twelve hours later, since all of us liked to sleep long.

The arrival of a new day announced itself by a cacophony of coughing. Eskimos have a rather weak bronchial system. Most of them smoke heavily, which doesn't improve it, and they are subject to the most violent and prolonged coughing fits, especially in the morning. After hawking and gasping for some time, Akpaleeapik pulled himself a bit out of his sleeping bag, pumped up and lit the Primus and soon a wonderful warmth spread through the tent.

He filled the teapot with ice chips and put it on the Primus, while Iseechee and I, lazy and cosy in our bags, pretended to be sound asleep, "awaking" only when we could hear the tea boil. Still in the bags, propped up on our elbows, we slurped the hot, sweet tea, two or three mugs each, dawdling deliciously, with none of that horrid early morning hustle and bustle of white man's expeditions. Now the tent was warm, I crawled out of my bag and, still in socks and underwear, made porridge, or fried piles of bacon and hardtack biscuits in its fat. After a few more mugs of tea and a leisurely pipe, we got dressed, willing to face a new day on the trail.

The tent was collapsed and rolled up, the boxes and sacks loaded on the sled, the snow shaken from the skins of our sleeping platform, the whole load was securely lashed down, the dogs were harnessed and on we went. It usually took two hours from the time we stopped until we were in bed, and an equal time from Akpaleeapik's first cough and until we were off.

CHAPTER FIVE

We continued to sledge west along the coast of Ellesmere Island. To our right the towering cliffs, striated in black and brown and sienna, soared skyward and in our path the snow glittered blindingly, each frozen flake seeming to catch the sun and reflect it in a dazzling burst of brilliance. We stopped frequently to check fox traps on shore, walking along raised, pebbly beaches, and running up narrow, V-shaped valleys, their rims ornamented with elegantly curlicued snow overhangs. In one trap we found a dead arctic hare. In this harsh land even hares become carnivorous and nibble at the blubber bait of traps.

It was warm in the sun. I could feel its intensity on my dark sledging pants, where the powdery snow thrown up by the trotting dogs changed into glistening droplets of ice to be slowly soaked up by the sun. Once the sun disappeared behind the mountains, it would become intensely cold. Now the mountains rose in sombre, jagged silhouette towards a dark blue sky streaked with delicate rose-red mare's-tail clouds.

The squeal of the sled runners on frozen snow rose higher and higher in pitch, harshly strident and dissonant, like the tuning up of an orchestra's string section. We crossed the wide mouth of Baad Fiord (Boat Fiord), where Sverdrup and some of his men had lived below an upturned boat when an early freeze-up caught them. Now it stretched—dusky blue—inland, flanked by black, forbidding mountains. Wind sprang up, the dogs trotted faster, my hands and feet turned numb and icy fingers of cold crept through my clothes. At first I ran, but as soon as I jumped off the sled the dogs began to gallop and, after a mad, exhausting dash, I threw myself on the sled again, gasping and still cold. After many unsuccessful tries at getting warm this way, I gave up and huddled in frigid misery atop my perch on the hamper. As if to mock

me, Goethe's lines of sun-drenched Italy shot into my mind:
Kennst du das Land wo die Citronen blühn,
Im dunkeln Laub die Gold-Orangen glühn,
Dahin, dahin lass uns Geliebter ziehn.

Know'st thou the land where the lemon trees bloom,
Where the gold orange glows in the deep thicket's gloom—
Thither, thither, my sweet one let us go.

We stopped after midnight in the lee of an iceberg. Akpaleeapik and Akeeagok walked back and forth, testing the snow, their iron harpoon shafts serving as probes. To build an igloo, the snow has to be of a certain consistency, otherwise the building blocks will fail to fuse and the whole structure may crumble.

Having found suitable snow, the brothers began to cut out blocks with handsaws. They sawed two parallel lines, about fifty inches apart, into a level stretch of snow, sectioned this off with transverse cuts every fourteen inches, undercut each block and lifted it out of the resulting trench. The blocks, about fifty, and weighing roughly forty pounds each, were slightly wedge-shaped and of amazing uniformity.

A first layer of blocks was set up in a large, perfect circle. A section of this circle was cut down in an oblique plane and on this the next layer was laid to circle upward and inward, in a continuous spiral. Akeeagok and I lugged the snow blocks up and put them in the appropriate spot, broad side down. Akpaleeapik, working inside the rising igloo, ran his broad-bladed snow knife between the new block and the ones already in place to create a smooth tactile surface, and pushed the new block into position, so it touched the snow block next to it and rested at a cant on the one below. As the walls rose higher, he increased the inward bevel of each block until, in apparent defiance of the law of gravity, the last blocks were lying nearly parallel to the floor below. At last only an irregularly shaped hole remained in the very centre of the snow-dome and into this Akpaleeapik fitted an appropriately cut cap-block.

Our igloo was complete. Nearly seven feet high in the centre and with a twelve-foot diameter at the bottom, it had taken just over an hour to build. The boys had been busy filling all chinks and interstices with loose snow and tamping it down. Now Akeeagok cut small steps into the blocks and climbed on top of the newly built igloo to fill all fissures there with snow. Akpaleeapik cut a low square door opening from the inside, pushed the block out and emerged on hands and knees.

We unloaded both sleds and passed pelts, sacks and boxes through the opening into the igloo. The boys chipped chunks of fresh-water ice from the berg and brought it in, the door-block was pushed into the igloo and finally we all crawled in. Before the stoves were lit, every bit of snow was carefully brushed from the furs of the sleeping platform, and from our clothes. This was our daily evening ritual, in igloo or tent, to avoid damp clothes and sleeping bags, which could not be dried out and, once humid, would no longer keep us warm.

Akeeagok pushed the snow block into the door opening, sealed all chinks with snow and we were immured in our white, windproof, vaulted home. The stoves were lit, soon the tea kettle hummed and a gargantuan stew bubbled busily in the pot; it became so warm, we stripped to our underwear and lolled lazily on the furs, smoking and talking. I dished out supper, being steward as well as cook, and we ate masses of it, then licked our plates and spoons, rinsed them with boiling water and wiped them clean with toilet paper. I had wondered at the outset, why Akpaleeapik insisted I take enough toilet tissue along to cope with a major diarrhoea epidemic. Now I realized its principal use was to serve as disposable dish towels.

I had always assumed an igloo to be a distinctly chilly abode. Actually the dry, new snow blocks are quite hygroscopic, absorb moisture like a sponge, and for a day, at least, the snow-house can be kept comfortably warm. Then the walls begin to glaze, lose their absorbency and, when the place is heated, drip, usually just above your head.

Replete after our immense meal, we drank a lot more tea, smoked and chatted, Akpaleeapik patiently repeating Eskimo words he had already explained to me and whose meaning I had again forgotten. We slipped into our sleeping bags, Akeeagok turned off the noisy pressure stoves, and silence descended upon our sugarcube house.

I was awakened by a low, monotonous mutter. Akeeagok, kneeling, but still in his sleeping bag, was reading his Bible (printed in England in cuneiform-looking Eskimo syllabics), rocking slightly back and forth like a Yeshiva student. It was early afternoon and Sunday. Outside the sun was shining, and our igloo was suffused with a soft, shadowless, greenish light.

I made breakfast. Akpaleeapik rummaged in one of the boxes and hauled out a transistor radio, carefully wrapped in a piece of caribou skin. It brought the wide world into our igloo: the Voice of America saying, in meticulously monotonous "special English," nasty things about Russia; Radio Moscow saying even nastier things about America; and an Oxford-Chinese voice of Radio Peking calling down a pox on both houses! Akpaleeapik listened to all versions of the Vietnam war with impartial equanimity, since he could understand none. It was the noise that mattered, and the pleasure of possessing the machine that made it. Henceforth Iseechee had to carry the radio batteries in an inside pocket in day-time and sleep with them at night, to keep them warm. I hated that radio, with its wildly contradictory messages from political messiahs around the globe, and was several times tempted to pinch one of the batteries. In the vastness of the Arctic, the radio brought into our tent or igloo, the "real" world. Yet to me, having to some extent returned to a form of primeval human existence, much of it sounded grotesque and unreal.

We stayed in the pit all day, eating, smoking, drinking tea, listening to that confounded radio and sleeping. The Eskimos' capacity for prolonged sleep is equalled by their ability to do without it, if necessary, for days and nights on end. It was 1 A.M. when we got up.

Outside it was cold and bleak. An ashen light lay on the land, completely shadowless, so one could neither judge distance nor see the alternating ridges and troughs of snow in our path and, when walking or running beside the sled, I continually stumbled against unseen obstacles or stepped into unnoticed holes and trenches.

The dogs were rested and eager, and we travelled fast to Muskox Fiord. There the men tethered both teams on the ice. "I will show you something," Akpaleeapik said, and off we went, through a maze of house-high ice blocks and upended floes, slipping and tripping in the shadowless light.

After two miles we came to a large, flat peninsula. Behind it a broad valley cleft the mountains. Near the tip of the peninsula, Akpaleeapik stopped. "Igloo!" he said, pointing to several dark objects ahead. In that deceptive light they still seemed a mile away. In fact, they were fifty yards from us: the remnants of a prehistoric Thule Eskimo settlement. There were about a dozen houses, circles of rock with a mass of large whale bones in their centre. These had once been walls, ribs and rafters of the houses. Now they were overgrown with black and orange lichen. Seeglook kicked some bones around in one of the houses, and emerged triumphant with a large polar bear skull, grey and pitted with age, but with its great curved canines still in place. Centuries ago, this had been a busy hunting camp; now it lay lonely and lifeless in the grey-yellow light.

On a peninsula in Muskox Fiord, Iseechee and Seeglook examine the remains of prehistoric Thule culture houses, built in part with the great bones of Greenland whales

Akpaleeapik and I walked back the way we had come. Akeeagok and the two boys preferred the easier walking of a raised beach. This gradually brought them, from river shelf to river shelf, to the rim of the valley. From there a snow-free ledge led farther and higher, and when they reached a final impasse they were a good four hundred feet above the fiord. Led by Akeeagok, they slid down the steep snow wall, first cautiously, kicking holds into the snow with their heels; but the last one hundred and fifty feet were nearly sheer — they glissaded down in gusts of snow and laughter and plunged pell-mell into a snowbank below.

We reached the brooding, crenellated mountain bastion of Cape Storm at noon. The boys stayed with the dogs, while Akpaleeapik and Akeeagok climbed the broad rock shelves at the foot of the cliff. On the highest ledge they lay down and scanned the icy vastness of Jones Sound with their telescopes, looking both for polar bears and for a good route through the tortuous maze of pressure ridges. I wandered about on the wide ledges and found several strange-looking structures, some small and square, built of large flat stone slabs; others seven feet tall and beehive-shaped, constructed of fairly small stones, with an opening at the top. After a couple of hours, when the brothers had finished their patient survey, I asked them about the stone structures.

"They are fox traps," Akpaleeapik said.

Near Cape Storm we also found several ancient beehive-shaped fox traps—a tilting stone at the top dumped the fox, attracted by bait, into the trap

We camped that night (3 P.M.!) in an old igloo near the base of Cape Storm. Akpaleeapik had built it two months before, while checking his trap line. It was small, and glazed inside, so it started to drip as soon as the pressure stoves spread some warmth. For a while we were busy plastering all the walls with long strips of toilet paper. The water drops soaked into the paper and seeped down the walls, instead of dripping on us. It worked quite well, but our igloo, papered in pink and yellow, looked most odd.

"How do you call the traps and how do they work?" I asked Akpaleeapik.

He was often taciturn, but he always cheered up when I questioned him about his land and his people, and liked to explain things to me with infinite patience. Now, drawing designs into the snow floor of our igloo with a fork handle, he told me about the Eskimos' ingenious traps of former days.

The small trap was called *pudlati.* It was built like a rectangular box with heavy stone slabs. Above its entrance hovered a flat stone, fitted into grooves on either side. From it a thong led to a chunk of bait in the rear of the trap. When a fox crawled in and pulled at the bait the entrance rock came crashing down, like the portcullis of a medieval castle, and the fox was imprisoned. Larger versions of the pudlati were used to capture wolves and even polar bears.

The beehive-shaped trap, Akpaleeapik said, was called *udlisau.* Into its two-foot opening at the top, a flat stone was inserted so that it could swivel. Sometimes a piece of polished ice was used instead. Just beyond the stone, or ice sheet, a chunk of meat was suspended as bait. When a fox climbed the udlisau and stepped on the swivel stone to reach the bait, it tipped forward and dumped him into the trap. Or he stepped on the polished ice and slid in. In either case, once inside, the fox could not possibly jump out of the high conical trap.

The Eskimos also used a deadfall to kill foxes before the days of steel traps.

"We called it *kangiak,*" Akpaleeapik explained. "First you made a hole in the ice. In the middle you left a little bump, like a woman's nipple. Above the hole you tilted a heavy sheet of ice and held it up with a stick, the lower end on the nipple. Then you tied some meat to the stick. The fox comes, pulls at the stick, the stick slips off the nipple, the ice falls down and the fox is dead."

But the most ingenious and cruel methods were devised to kill wolves. The wolf killers were called *issidjua* and *alukpa*.

"The issidjua was made of baleen," Akpaleeapik said. "You

sharpened narrow strips of baleen at both ends, coiled them into tight balls, tied them up with sinew and smeared them with blood and blubber. Then you dropped them outside. When wolves came along, they gulped down the balls. In their stomachs the sinew was digested, the coiled balls of baleen sprang apart, pierced their guts and they would die shortly thereafter. The Eskimos had only to follow their tracks and pick them up."

The alukpa was even worse. "To make an alukpa, the Eskimos only needed a piece of shin bone from a caribou," Akpaleeapik said. "They made one end as sharp as a knife. Later they also used knives they got from the whalers. They chipped a little hole into the ice, set the sharpened bone or knife into it, so that only a couple of inches stuck out and filled the hole with a mixture of blood and water. This would freeze right away. When a wolf came along, he smelled the blood and started to lick it. But he cut his tongue on the sharp bone and bled and the warm blood made him excited and he licked and bled and licked and bled, and bled until he died."

We slept until midnight and emerged from our leaky igloo into an intensely cold, bleak, blustery day, the second of May. The sleds were turned upside down and the runners coated with flour paste, prepared over the Primus in a special pot. The paste-surfaced runners were smoothed with a file. Akpaleeapik told me to boil a kettle of water, poured some of it into a can and added snow until the water was tepid. Then he spread water on the runners with a tuft of polar bear skin, and it frozen instantly into an even layer of ice. This he smoothed with his snow knife until not the slightest ridge remained on the runners' polished surface.

The sleds were loaded, the dogs harnessed and we headed south across Jones Sound towards Devon Island. Fine drifting snow enveloped us like a floating veil. The great mountains of Ellesmere vanished behind us and we drove on and on, with white above, white below and white all around, skirting enormous pressure ridges, until I hypnotized myself into believing we were travelling in endless circles, going on forever and ever, from nowhere to nowhere, in this vistaless land of white.

I nudged Akpaleeapik. "How do you know which way to go?" I asked. He smiled, amused at my ignorance.

"The prevailing wind on Jones Sound is from east to west," he explained. "So the snow drifts run east-west. And we go from north to south. As long as we travel across the snow drifts, and not alongside them, we are heading south."

It was, at times, like travelling over an endless washboard with ripples four to eight feet high. We sledged across a brief flat stretch, to come to a high snow drift. The dogs rushed up and over, pulling with all their strength; the sled rose steeply up and up, its nose pointing skyward, teetered for an instant on the crest and came crashing down on the far side with a spine-jarring bang. Akpaleeapik on one side and Iseechee on the other pushed and pulled the sled each time to the best approach and guided it over the hump, while I perched fairly useless on my hamper, trying not to fall off, or when I did, to get back on quickly.

Sometimes, though, the walls of a snowdrift were too steep and, instead of gliding up, the runners buried themselves in its side. We were pitched off the sled by the abrupt halt, while on the far side of the drift, the huskies, yanked to a stop, were blaming Apapak for this mishap. They ganged up on him, and the air was full of his desperate soprano trill. Iseechee scrambled up on the crest of the drift and yelled at the dogs, who blithely ignored him, while Akpaleeapik and I strained to pull the sled back and push it upwards the moment the dogs threw themselves into harness. Often the sled would dig in again and we had to get the shovel and dig a sloping passage into the drift.

After many hours of this roller-coaster progress—from trough to crest, and crest to trough, get stuck, dig out and sledge on—I was tired and fed up. The Eskimos seemed neither tired nor annoyed. They faced each new obstacle with equanimity, dug out the sled if it impaled itself in a drift, and when, after a while, it got really bad it only seemed to strike Akpaleeapik as funny.

There is an essential difference in the approach to arctic travel between Eskimos and white men. To the white man it is a form of personal combat with an alien, hostile environment. When all goes well, which rarely happens, the white man is quite happy. But when pressure ridges, leads of open water or other obstacles bar his path, he looks at them as a challenge to be overcome, hence the strong dramatization of most accounts of arctic travel. The Eskimos tackles the same obstacles routinely. To him the white vastness is not an alien hostile environment: it is his homeland. If mile after mile of steep-walled snow drifts bar the way, that is to be expected on such a trip and he gets neither flustered nor annoyed.

We finally extricated ourselves from the pleated, parallel lines of drifts and sledged over fairly smooth ice and snow, in the mat, fulvous light of a sun which never quite managed to break through the clouds. Suddenly, ghost-like and silent, a flock of fulmars skimmed over the ice, and banked past us on ash grey wings.

Related to shearwaters and petrels, the fulmars are common in the Arctic and look rather like compact, thick-necked gulls. I had often seen them in summer, gliding with stiff wings over wave crests and down into troughs, banking steeply, the downward wing tip within inches of the water, and soaring effortlessly up over the next crest. In summer they often follow ships and boats, and now they slid silently back and forth above our canine caravan, glided into a trough between snow ridges, banked sharply and came swooping back over us.

Akpaleeapik threw his mitt into the air and, as a fulmar swept low towards it, he tried to hook it out of the air with his thirty-foot whip. But the bird evaded the lashing rawhide with ease. Our dogs, alarmed by the hiss of the dreaded whip, broke into a gallop and poor Iseechee, off to retrieve his father's mitten, had to run like hell to catch up with our sled.

CHAPTER SIX

It was noon when we came across the fresh polar bear tracks. For the past hour I had been peeking surreptitiously at my watch, hoping we'd camp soon. It was twelve hours since we had had a meal, and I felt cold, hungry, and disgruntled. Now we changed course abruptly to follow the great plantigrade spoor in the snow. Both brothers stood on their pitching sleds, balancing with bent knees, to scan the ice ahead.

Suddenly Akeeagok saw the bear and, in the same instant, the bear winded us and took off in a rolling, ungainly gallop. In feverish haste, Akeeagok freed six of his dogs, grabbed his rifle and ran after the bear.

We dumped the entire load off Akeeagok's sled, hitched our team to it so that it was pulled by twenty-three dogs who, being from rival teams, immediately started a fur-flying free-for-all—until Akpaleeapik waded into the mass of snarling, ripping dogs and laid out left and right with the stout wooden handle of his whip. The dogs screamed with fright, and jumped forward. Akpaleeapik leapt nimbly out of the traces and threw himself on the sled as it raced by.

The bear headed for a vast area of pressure ice—miles upon miles of ice blocks, some twenty feet high, the spaces between filled with belly-deep powdery snow. Akeeagok was already far ahead, running, slipping, falling, floundering through deep, soft snow, scrambling over the steep, hard snow drifts that ran like sharp, triangular ribs from the lee of each upended ice floe.

Up raced the dogs, wild with excitement, and up tilted the sled, while we clung to it, desperately. It teetered on a crest and plunged down, slipping sideways against ice blocks, turned over, was righted again, but never stopped. When we fell off, we did not let go of the sled, but dragged along, blinded by flying snow, and pulled ourselves up on the madly bucking sled again. My knee got crushed between

51

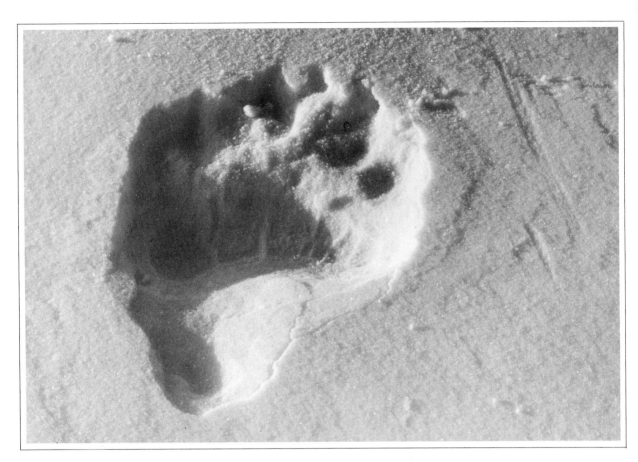

The great plantigrade spoor of the polar bear—it lured us on in a wild ride through pressure ice

the racing sled and a block of ice, and I could feel it swell and stiffen. Once I was flung head-forward down a deep hole, when the sled turned over on top of an ice block, and Akpaleeapik yanked me out by the legs. But we did not stop.

Hour after hour we raced through the crazy jumble of ice blocks, traces snagging, dogs screaming with fear, being hauled back under the runners of the heavy sled. But on we went, ever on. Akeeagok, racing ahead like a man obsessed, shed parka, pullover, sledging pants and mitts as he ran, and we scooped them up in passing and tied them to the thwarts of the sled. Once three dogs reached the bear, but he turned on them in fury. They fell back, and the bear lumbered on, his long claws digging like crampons into the ice, his rubber-like, skidproof soles preventing him from slipping.

After five hours we reached an open area in the ice field and caught up with Akeeagok, his sweat-soaked head wreathed in a cloud of steam. He slumped onto the sled, and in the icy wind the sweat froze into a hoarfrost mask, his soaked shirt turned into icy armour. By the time he had dressed again, we reached new fields of pressure ice. Now Akpaleeapik and the boys took turns running ahead, while Akeeagok tried to steer the sled through this maze of jagged ice blocks, following the great spoor in a nearly monomaniac frenzy of exictement.

My role in the wild hunt through the chaotic ice, was entirely passive: clinging to the sled, trying not to get too seriously hurt, hoping against hope that the cameras might survive, and cursing viciously bears, Eskimos and ice. The sled pitched over a hundred times, was righted again and we flung ourselves on in a pile, pulling in our legs at the same instant, not to get them crushed between the sled and the next ice blocks. Traces tangled and snapped, and were retied on the run, and on we went, ever on, with *Ça ira mal!* *Ça ira mal!* throbbing through my aching head in a deadly refrain.

We continued the wild chase for another five hours. Then they gave up. The bear was far ahead. We slumped down on the sled, utterly exhausted. The dogs lay still, too tired, for once, to fight. My knee was now so swollen, I could feel its pressure against my baggy pants. In the mad rush I hadn't even taken my pipe along.

"Akeeagok, give me a cigarette," I asked.

He fished out a badly crushed package from his shirt pocket, moist with sweat. We smoked in silence. I guess we all thought the same thing. Somewhere, forty or fifty miles away, in that phantasmagoric chaos of ice were our tents, our sleeping bags, our food, our stoves, everything we needed to survive. We had to make the long trip back.

It was a dismal journey. The dogs were nearly finished. They would not go unless one of us walked ahead. Their tails, normally cockily curled on their backs, now drooped. They ignored the usually much feared whip. The moment we all sat on the sled, they lay down, thirstily scooping up gobs of snow. Akeeagok and Akpaleeapik whipped them mercilessly. They howled and cringed, but would not budge.

We skirted the enormous fields of pressure ice, one of us stumbling ahead in a stupor of hunger and fatigue, while the others huddled together on the sled and slept, on and on, throughout the grim grey night and most of the next day. Only Apapak felt fine. He had torn his trace, nearly at the beginning of the hunt, and had cagily followed the sled from a distance, never coming close enough to be caught and reharnessed. Now he played lead dog, running ahead, stopping every once in a while to look back, waiting for us to catch up and then prancing proudly ahead. Normally the huskies would have pounced on him in unanimous fury, but now they just walked along, tired and apathetic, moving mechanically as long as the man in front of them moved, and lying down the instant he stopped.

It was evening by the time we found the other sled and the scattered equipment. For once the usually so meticulous and methodical Eskimos were slipshod. They tethered and fed the dogs in a hurry; we set up the tents, drank mug after mug of tea, gulped down little chunks of raw, frozen seal meat they still had along from Grise Fiord, crawled into our sacks and passed out.

I woke up twelve hours later to a frightful racket. It was storming outside and the tents were fluttering wildly in the wind. Akpaleeapik was getting dressed. I crept out of the sack, aching all over, the knee still swollen and extremely painful and pulled on my clothes. Fine snow was filtering into the tent. It probably was not more than ten below, but with that biting wind it felt more like forty below. Akpaleeapik began to cut snow blocks and built with them a five-foot-high windbreak around the tent.

A baleful, dull-orange sun was slanting across the snow ridges—their crests ochre, the troughs deep violet. Long streamers of roseate, powdery snow raced and danced with the wind. It looked beautiful, but cold and lonely. The dogs lay tightly curled, noses hidden under bushy tails, their fur powdered with snow. I took some pictures. My hands quickly numbed, but I was grateful the cameras still seemed to work well after our wild sleigh ride. I crawled back into the tent, made a big pot of porridge and lots of tea, since we still felt parched and dehydrated. We ate and drank and went back to sleep for another twelve hours, while the storm moaned and whistled around the snow block rampart outside.

The storm had blown itself out when we emerged next morning. Our sleds were buried in a drift. Little mounds of snow began to stir here and there, and our dogs peered out through masks of snow-covered hair. It took us a couple of hours to dig out the camp. We sledged on, giving the pressure ice a wide berth. I perched on my hamper, my derrière still feeling as if it had been ground to hamburger.

We stopped near a towering twin-peaked iceberg, one spire rising needle-sharp towards the dark blue sky, the other truncated, so that from a distance the berg looked a shimmering frozen replica of the Rouen cathedral. This distinctively shaped iceberg was an old acquaintance of Akeeagok's, and he told me a long story about its peregrinations during the last eight years: "In 1962 it was not far from Grise Fiord and I shot a seal near it. Last year it was near the coast of Devon Island, about seventy miles from here. Three years ago I was chasing a big bear and, just when I thought I would lose him, he headed for this berg and climbed right on top of it. The dogs could not follow. They jumped like crazy at the base of the berg, yapping and howling, and the bear sat on top and hissed at them, until I came up and shot him and he came tumbling down, bang! right between the dogs!"

Akpaleeapik and Akeeagok chipped steps into the steep wall of the berg with their snow knives and climbed to its summit. There they sat for hours, dark statues on a gigantic white pedestal, scanning the ice and snow of Jones Sound for polar bear. I tried to follow them, but the icy wall was so steep and the smooth leather soles of my kamiks so slippery I lost my nerve halfway up and cautiously climbed down again. Throughout the trip I never ceased to marvel at the self-assured ease with which the Eskimos climbed the nearly perpendicular ice walls of any berg they wished to use as lookout.

In the evening we set up camp near another berg, some fifteen miles from the Devon Island coast. While I cooked supper, the brothers climbed the berg for another long and chilly survey with their telescopes.

Iseechee poked his head into the tent.

"My father calls you," he said.

I clambered up the berg, clinging to the holds chipped into the ice. Akpaleeapik motioned me to the telescope, cradled in a grooved snow block.

"Look," he said.

Far out amidst the whiteness I could just discern a yellowish speck.

"Nanook [polar bear]," Akpaleeapik said, a slight tremor of excitement in his usually quiet voice. "Nanook sleep. We eat first. Then we hunt."

I bolted my food, but the Eskimos ate slowly, drank tea and seemed not the least concerned, while I had visions of the polar bear trotting off into the sunset.

"Will the bear not go away?" I asked Akpaleeapik.

"No," he said. "He sleeps now. He will start to walk later, at night, when it gets very cold."

This time the hunt was carefully prepared. Akeeagok kept watching the bear, while Akpaleeapik iced the sled runners, lashed layers of soft caribou pelts and the polar bear skin on the sled, and tied a box with Primus stove, tea kettle and some food on the back of the sled.

Like a statue atop the iceberg, Akeeagok scans the vastness of Jones Sound for polar bear

Facing page:
Akeeagok climbs a great iceberg in Jones Sound to look for polar bear from its peak

We harnessed the dogs. Akeeagok climbed down from the berg.

"Nanook walks that way," he said, motioning eastward.

The guns were slipped under the lashing ropes and the dogs lunged forward. It was 11 P.M. and twenty below zero. The snow underneath the runners squealed shrilly, like a hundred off-key violins. And just above the horizon hung a malevolently yellow sun, cold and cheerless. We skirted icebergs and great jumbles of pressure ice. The dogs ran fast, sensing somehow the suppressed excitement of their masters. We were circling to leeward of the bear, so he could not smell us.

We were half a mile away when we spotted the bear, walking leisurely across the ice in his peculiar shuffling gait. The dogs smelled him and broke into a wild gallop. Stradding the racing sled like a sulky-driver, Akpaleeapik pulled in the traces and unhooked the first dogs to stream after the bear. Alarmed by the noise, the bear stopped, peered nearsightedly in our direction and, suddenly aware of his danger, fled in an ungainly but fast gallop.

"Oorooroorooroooo!" screamed Akpaleeapik, high-pitched and wild, and on raced our remaining dogs, our sled tossing and slewing like a boat in a storm. Akeeagok released some of his dogs, they raced past us and our sled chased them. The first dogs had caught up with the bear, darted in to attack and dashed back when the bear turned on them.

Finally fifteen dogs, in a frenzy of excitement, danced around their lumbering foe and held the bear at bay. Akpaleeapik shouted. Both men released their last dogs and we raced after them on foot, stumbling and slipping on ice blocks, in the weird yellowish light of the midnight sun. Akpaleeapik shot and missed. The bear broke through the circle of yelping dogs and galloped off but, beset from all sides, stopped again on a small snow mound, swatting at the dogs with his paws or making short charges, his mouth agape. Around him the twenty-nine dogs darted in, and dashed back, raising puffs of powdery snow that glittered golden against the sun.

This time Akpaleeapik ran to within a few feet of the bear. He shot, the bear rolled backwards, rose with a snarl and tried to charge. Akpaleeapik shot again at point-blank range, a convulsive shudder shook the massive form, then it lay still.

The men reeved a thong through a hole cut into the bear's upper lip, tied the dogs' traces to this warp and dragged their prize back to the sleds. We heaved the bear onto Akpaleeapik's long sled and drove back to camp. While I made tea, the Eskimos skinned the bear and spread the skin out on the snow. They quartered the carcass,

A husky skips nimbly away as the enraged polar bear charges

and fed some of the meat and guts to the dogs, taking care to cut out and hide the liver. Polar bear liver is so rich in vitamin A, it is poisonous. Men who eat it can die of hypervitaminosis.

"If dogs eat polar bear liver, they get sick and lose their hair," Akpaleeapik said, then with a wink at my bald top asked: "Maybe you eat polar bear liver sometime?"

We had a big pot of polar bear stew. I was glad to be cook, since polar bear meat can be infested with trichina, the parasite that causes the painful and sometimes fatal trichinosis. I boiled the meat thoroughly, adding salt, much to the Eskimos' chagrin. The stringy meat had a strong, gamy flavour. The Eskimos ate chunks of boiled blubber with the meat, but I could manage only a few small cubes. The night was bitterly cold. When I tried to write, the pencil refused to work. Somehow I had never expected a pencil to freeze, but it would not write until I had warmed it up over the Primus stove.

The hunters pull a killed bear to their sleds

Akeeagok begins to skin the bear he shot

We were camped on the ice of Bear Bay, so named by Sverdrup's men in honour of the nanook who, seventy years ago had been numerous here: ". . . [it] must be a favourite haunt of the bears, for there were tracks nearly everywhere; in certain places literally beaten tracks."

My Eskimos, too, hoped to see more bears in this bay. They were up on the berg before I awoke, scanning mile after mile of ice and snow, tears trickling from straining eyes, leaving briny white tracks down their cheeks.

The dogs had eaten half the bear and slept replete and content in the snow. They were always tethered to a long chain, the ends of which were anchored in the ice, two together every six feet in a strict, hierarchical order, each pair consisting of dogs of nearly equal social status. Apapak, of course, was tied up all by himself at the far end of the chain, well out of snapping distance of the nearest husky.

After breakfast, we lashed only the furs and the "tea boxes"—with Primus, kettle and a bag of hardtack—onto the sleds and drove east, keeping on the ice some ten miles from the Devon Island shore. It was eight days since we had left Grise Fiord, yet somehow it seemed like months ago. Time had lost its meaning; days and nights, now nearly equally bright, melted into each other, and my orderly city life seemed incredibly remote and rather unreal, like a vague dream. Only the sled was real, and the snow and the ice, the searing wind and the endless white, and the stench that wafted back to us from the farting dogs, still bloated with polar bear meat.

The dogs were full and lazy, but suddenly they spotted something in the snow, and sheared off at right angles in a gallop, nearly overturning the sled. It was a seal carcass, nearly stripped of blubber and meat by the polar bear who had scooped the luckless pinniped out of its breathing hole. Our dogs fell upon it as if they hadn't eaten in years, Akeeagok's team rushed up and leapt into the fray and in an instant the twenty-nine dogs were massed into a ball, tearing at the seal and at each other, intertwining their traces, and, from the midst of canine mayhem, rose the terrified screams of Apapak. We dashed in, kicking and lashing at the dogs, grabbing them by their long fur and tossing them aside, and finally extricated from this melee of furry fiends an unhurt, but utterly hysterical Apapak.

We zigzagged from iceberg to iceberg. The brothers climbed up, looked patiently but in vain for polar bears and on we went to the next berg.

We stopped for tea near a magnificent blue-green iceberg shaped in the elegant lines of a Viking ship. Just ahead lay Cape Svarten, which Sverdrup's men had named after Svarten (Blacky), one of their most remarkable dogs. They had sledged along the north Devon Island shore in the spring of 1902. Near this cape a polar bear "crept up to within a few paces of the dogs under the lee of some hummocks, and when the team observed it they sang out, broke loose, and gave chase." The dogs failed to stop the bear and in the course of the day returned to camp. Only Svarten did not reappear. They sledged on without him, continued their survey of the coast until they were stopped by pressure ridges, and returned to their basecamp near the shore of Ellesmere Island. And there, two weeks later, Svarten turned up again, smug and round; but what he had done, and what or whom he had eaten in the interval, they never found out.

There were many polar bear tracks near our berg. I asked Akpaleeapik how long he and his brother would stay on the mountain looking for bear. About two hours, he thought.

"Then I'll follow the tracks of a bear for a while and see what he does," I said.

"Okay, we'll pick you up with the dogs," Akpaleeapik said.

The spoor I followed must have been left by a large bear: each track measured a good twelve inches in diameter. At first it seemed as if the bear had been on an aimless amble, but soon a purposeful patrol pattern emerged. The bear had wandered from one frozen-in iceberg to the next. Approaching them from leeward, he had circled each berg, paying particular attention to the huge, wind-fluted snowdrifts. I had seen Akpaleeapik and Akeeagok check these drifts, probing them with their harpoon shafts.

"Sometime you find *nunarjaks* below them," Akpaleeapik explained. These are the oval lairs ringed seal mothers excavate under snowdrifts as nurseries for their pups, who are born with a long, white, silky-soft foetal fur coat. Until they moult it, at the age of three or four weeks, they cannot seek safety in the sea, since the natal coat becomes waterlogged and they sink. If the bear can find them—and with his acute sense of smell he can detect them through five feet of snow—they are easy prey.

At the fourth berg the spoor told of success. Great chunks of compacted snow had been scooped from a drift, and the bear had broken through the ice-coated roof of the seal's lair. Two limp, furry flippers in the snow were all that remained of the pup. A mile farther, the bear had climbed a small berg. He must have spotted a seal from this lookout, since the great plantigrade tracks led straight

64

from the berg to a nearby pressure ridge. In its shelter the bear had trotted along, to a point nearest the seal. There he had emerged from between the ice blocks and for 150 yards the snow looked as if someone had dragged a large heavy sack over it.

"The bear creeps along flat on the ice," Akpaleeapik told me later. With his telescope, he has several times seen bears stalking seal. "He pulls himself forward with his front paws and presses with his back paws. The moment the seal wakes up, he puts a paw over his black nose and stops. The seal looks all around, but he sees nothing. So he goes back to sleep. And then the bear crawls forward again."

At about ten yards from the breathing hole, the signs in the snow showed the bear had hunched himself up, and deeply imprinted, widely spaced and rather slurred tracks told of a lightning rush upon the sleeping seal.

The bear may have only eaten the blubber, his favourite food, but his retinue of arctic foxes had neatly stripped the meat off the bones. Their small tracks dotted the snow all around. Nearly invariably when we found polar bear tracks, we also saw the imprints of foxes nearby, following their shaggy lord in hope of leftovers.

The snow reflected the spring sun with scorching intensity and I was glad when Akpaleeapik came to fetch me. The dogs, seeing a dark figure in the distance, galloped as if possessed and I had to jump aside not to be run over by the whole pack of overeager huskies.

"Too warm," Akpaleeapik said. "Nanook sleep. We go back." Polar bears, he explained, don't like to wander about when it is so warm. They flake out on some ice block and snooze in the sun. Our dogs, too, didn't like the warmth. It was still probably a few degrees below zero, but in the sun it felt warm. Tongues lolling, they slowly trotted back towards our tents, but perked up when they noticed something in the snow some distance away. It was the carcass of a polar bear. Enveloped in pink blubber, the flayed body looked somehow obscenely naked.

"*Innuit* [Eskimos] from Resolute Bay shoot bear," Akpaleeapik said. "They come by skidoo. Take only the pelt." For the meat these motorized hunters have no use. They kill the bears only for their pelts, worth to them, on the average, a hundred and eighty to two hundred dollars. We kicked the dogs away from the carcass, rolled it on our sled, and drove it back to camp. Like the polar bear, we were both hunters and scavengers. A polar bear carcass left by other hunters, or a partially eaten seal left by a bear, were always welcome, since we needed piles of meat to feed our ravenous huskies. The great slabs of walrus meat and blubber Akeeagok had taken along on his sled from Grise Fiord were finished; and to feed the dogs and ourselves we now needed at least a hundred pounds of meat each day.

CHAPTER SEVEN

Akpaleeapik was sick. He had a stomach complaint and had severely strained himself in the ruthless hunt through the pressure ice. Now he sat morosely in the tent, burping and eating sodium bicarbonate, retching and wretched. Ageeagok was deeply worried. He endeavoured to anticipate his brother's every wish and worked harder than ever. I made polar bear broth, and we both tried to persuade Akpaleeapik to just lie in his bag and rest. But he couldn't and wouldn't. Like many Eskimos, he is a nearly compulsive worker. Now he hauled all the dogteam traces into the tent and began to repair them. Most had been torn in the mad chase through the pressure ice and the ends had been hurriedly knotted or, at best, joined with a cut splice. Akpaleeapik undid all the knots, scarfed the torn thong ends with his little penknife and sewed them together with thread made of sinew. This task finished, he turned to his and Iseechee's footwear, cut off the soles of caribou-skin socks whose fur had become matted from sweating and walking, and deftly sewed new pieces of fluffy, warm caribou fur in place.

For himself and Iseechee he carried a whole bag of outer and inner boots along, to suit every weather and snow condition. On cold, drifting days, he wore kamiks shafted with polar bear skin, on which the snow does not melt. When it was cold and dry, kamiks with a ringed seal shaft were preferred, and for wet days he had several different pairs of waterproof kamiks, made of dark, oil-treated leather.

He was brusque and annoyed when Akeeagok and I fussed over him, feeling, no doubt, the deep resentment of a strong-willed, forceful man whose body is sapped by sickness. His face became haggard with pain, but the worse he felt, the more ruthlessly he drove himself. He may also have felt an atavistic fear of illness, for in past ages, when a hunter was gravely sick or maimed in this land without mercy, it must have been like a horribly humbling sentence of death. The Arctic before the days of nursing stations and planes that whisk a sick man south to a hospital, was a land of the strong and the healthy, and the spectre of weakening illness must have haunted each hunter. Since old age and illness were an inevitable part of life, they were, no doubt, accepted with a good deal of fatalism, but deep down, in his innermost self, the Eskimo must have felt a lurking fear of both. And Akpaleeapik, the proud and powerful hunter, refused to give in or spare himself, no matter how miserable he felt.

Akpaleeapik took out a map from a box and showed me the route he proposed to take across Devon Island, from Thomas Lee Inlet on the north coast to Maxwell Bay, off Lancaster Sound. None of the Grise Fiord or Resolute Bay Eskimos had ever crossed the island at this spot, but Akpaleeapik was optimistic.

"One sleep," he predicted, meaning we would make the overland journey in two days and one night. He drank his bear broth, and many mugs of tea, and smoked cigarette after cigarette, hoping to ease the pain. A strident pop voice wailed from the radio and outside the huskies howled in counterpoint.

It was warm and muggy next day. A uniform, luminous, skim-milk blue haze hung over ice and land. The ice was a great deal smoother than it had been sixty-six years ago when the disgruntled Norwegian sledgers named the high, scree-banked bluff at the entrance to Thomas Lee Inlet, Skruis Point—Pressure Ice Point. The snow was soft and wet, and groaned petulantly under the runners of the long sleds. Through the bluish veil we could see the steep-sided, fluted mountains on either side of the inlet, snow-filled, V-shaped rifts alternating with dark rock ribs in a backgammon-board pattern. The dogs strained in harness, hauling the sleds through the moist, yielding, sticky snow.

Akpaleeapik spotted a seal in the distance and we stopped. He watched the animal for a long time through binoculars and then prepared to stalk it. From his hunting bag, tied to the front of the sled where he kept spare ammunition, maps, telescope and binoculars, he took out a large rectangular sheet of white cloth with small, triangular pockets at each corner. Into these pockets he inserted two sticks, diagonally across the sheet to hold it taut. A third stick, its end capped with a white handkerchief, was pushed into the centre of the sheet, so it bulged out like a buckler, and tied where all three sticks intersected. Its projecting end served as handle. He checked his gun and walked towards the seal, sleeping on the ice some three hundred yards away, next to its breathing hole.

Akeeagok observes a sleeping seal while standing on the sled and steadying his telescope with his harpoon shaft

Akpaleeapik readies the white hunting screen used to stalk seal across the flat ice

Crouching behind the screen, Akpaleeapik takes aim the moment the seal has fallen asleep

The seal, shot through the head, lies dead near its breathing hole. While Akpaleeapik rests from the long stalk the boys make room on the sled for the seal.

The ringed seal is a fitful sleeper. It suddenly raises its head, looks carefully all round for ten or fifteen seconds and, if all seems safe, slumps down and sleeps for a minute or less. Akpaleeapik walked around the seal in a wide circle, to approach it from downwind. Then he started his stealthy stalk. Each time the seal moved, he ducked behind the whiteness of his portable screen. As soon as the seal started to sleep, he walked quickly towards it, his steps noiseless in the soft snow. When he was fifty yards from the seal, he waited until the animal had finished its cautious survey of the snowy plain around and slumped down to sleep again, then he took careful aim over his shield, and we heard the faint crack of his rifle. Through the binoculars I saw the seal hump convulsively, and then lie still. It had been shot through the head. In this hunt the shot must kill instantly, or the seal, even if fatally wounded, will slip down the hole beside which it lies and will be lost.

Our dogs had followed their master's stalk with keen interest. The moment they heard the rifle they raced off so fast I missed my sled and had just time to throw myself on Akeeagok's sled as it shot past. When we arrived, Akpaleeapik had already dismantled his shield, folded the cloth carefully and put it back into its plastic bag. In past ages, the Eskimos used similar shields made of bleached caribou leather.

We lashed the dead seal onto Akeeagok's sled. It got even warmer as the day advanced, the air was white and liquid as milk, the light even and intense. I took a reading with my light metre and it nearly snapped the needle off. The runners sank deep into the sticky snow, the dogs panted and padded along in droopy lassitude, and when the command came to stop they dropped in their tracks.

Akpaleeapik and Akeeagok skinned the seal, slit it open and, squatting in the snow beside it, cut off pieces of still-warm liver and meat, and ate it together with snippets of blubber.

"Have some," Akpaleeapik said.

Feeling slightly revolted, I took some liver, warm and slippery with blood, and swallowed it. It was the idea of eating raw liver that made me gag, because the taste wasn't bad, and after a while I managed to get more down and even to enjoy it, especially the rather bland, slightly sweetish blubber. Akeeagok ripped out some intestines, slit them open and ate their lining. Soon we looked like a triptych of original man, a trio squatting over the warm carcass on the snow's white table cloth, ripping out guts and liver, our hands and faces smeared with blood.

The word Eskimo is derived from an Algonquian Indian name

Akeeagok cuts up the seal for the dogs—Akpaleeapik and the boys build our igloo for the night

meaning "eaters of raw meat," an opprobrious term the Indians pinned on their neighbours to the north whom they thoroughly disliked. The Eskimos refer to themselves proudly as *Innuit*—Man, pre-eminent. To eat meat, blubber and innards raw was an utter necessity to a people living on a nearly exclusive meat diet. Only this way could they get the vitamins to keep them healthy. And what the body craves, the taste buds in some manner approve. During the next weeks, as we ran out of canned food and lived increasingly and finally entirely on meat, I began to look forward to eating some of it raw and developed a near-craving for raw blubber. What started as a gesture to please my hosts, and in order not to appear a silly sissy, ended up as an at least temporarily acquired taste.

It was snowing next morning. Gusts of wind raced up the inlet and we drove off into a whirling whiteness. At the head of the inlet we came up against a nearly solid wall of ice, thrown up in wild confusion in the tidal zone. While the boys looked after the dogs the brothers and I squeezed our way through the ice blocks and climbed the shelving shore nearby, to look from there for a feasible route through the ice. Akpaleeapik and Akeeagok sat down to scan the ice ahead with binoculars during lulls between gusts of snow, and I wandered about, glad to be on land again after spending more than a week on ice.

It was a bleak and forlorn place: bare frost-cracked dull brown rocks and dark shingle, covered occasionally by a dull, desiccated growth of lichen. The snow grew denser, swirling around in eddies and filtering into my goggles. And suddenly, through the wind-whipped curtain of snow trilled a gay little song, a cheerful chirrupy chatter, ending in a high clear whistle of pure delight, a supremely happy spirit singing in a dead and frozen world. It was a snow bunting on its way to its far-north breeding area. I looked for the little bird, but could not find it in the driving snow. The Eskimos got up and walked back to the sleds, and as I followed them the wind carried snatches of the bunting's jubilant song to me.

It took us hours to cross the ice barrier, guiding the heavily loaded sleds over the jagged ice blocks and righting them when they over-turned. From the beach we sledged inland on the blue-black ice of a frozen river, the sleds clattering along at great rate, the dogs scrabbling and slipping, and Apapak, poor lummox, falling flat on his face every ten yards.

Farther up the valley, the river had cut a deep, now snow-filled trough, and we followed its meandering course into a strange boreal fairy-tale land. The walls on either side of the valley rose in steep scree slopes to three hundred feet and then soared as nearly perpendicular cliffs to heights of six hundred to one thousand feet, their tops carved into giant cornices of a weirdly eroded sculpture. Seen through the veil of drifting snow, great dark turrets and crenelated bartizans seemed to tower above the valley, pierced and machicolated battlements, and slim, single columns of stone gazed like petrified sentinels down on our little procession. The snow became deeper and softer, the dogs sank in to their bellies and, although we now plodded alongside, they could barely haul the heavy sleds.

When we stopped for tea, Akeeagok and Akpaleeapik trimmed with scissors the long fur sprouting between the dogs' pads, now balling up with soft, sticky snow. Some dogs submitted to this perfectly painless procedure with the resigned look of long-suffering martyrs. But most screamed as if they were about to be flayed alive. They did not fight their masters or snap, but accompanied the whole operation with one sustained ear-splitting screech.

Wet, soft snow bunches up with the long fur underneath the dogs' paws, so Akeeagok trims the hair. Some dogs howled and struggled, others, like his lead dog here, endured the operation with quiet resignation.

The valleys widened into a rock-strewn maze of rounded banks and sledging became nearly impossible. The moment the runners struck earth or rock, we were stuck. Iseechee ran forward to pick up the dogs' traces, hauled them up and let go suddenly. The dogs sprang ahead, we heaved with all our strength, the sled jerked forward over the rocks with a nasty grating noise, only to get stuck on another earth ridge a few yards farther. It took us three hours to cover a mile.

We rested the dogs, and Akpaleeapik and Akeeagok reconnoitred one side of the valley, which was sloping up, not too steeply here, to a plateau. They found it adequately covered with snow, and we hitched all twenty-nine dogs to one sled, quelled some furious fights with kicks and curses, and sledged obliquely up the mountain, Akpaleeapik running along shouting "Aie! Aie! Aie!" to encourage the dogs, and whipping them for good measure, while the rest of us helped to haul the sled. On top, we untied the dogs and went to get the other sled.

Heading for Devon Island on a sunny day, the dogs are preceded by their shadows

Travelling inland on Devon Island, we follow the twisting course of a river valley

The joy of sledging on snow again was fairly short-lived. After a couple of hours we realized the plateau was getting increasingly narrow, falling off on both sides to river valleys, and finally we came to its end where the valleys met.

The dogs looked down the steep snow slope and backed off in unanimous fear. But the Eskimos were in no mood to sledge back and find some easy route down. Akpaleeapik and Akeeagok lined up one sled on the rim, while the dogs howled dolefully. This, they realized, was going to be damned unpleasant. Akpaleeapik and Iseechee clung to the sled on either side and Akeeagok and I shoved it over the edge. After braking frantically with outstretched legs for some moments, father and son let go, rolling helter-skelter down the hill. The dogs raced for their life, howling with fear as the great sled leapt after them. All might have gone well had not Apapak glanced back at the hurtling monster, tripped—and the next instant the sled was on him, buried him and dragged him, screeching, downwards. The huskies scattered to let the sled pass, some were run over and all were zipped through a cloud of flying snow by the runaway sled.

Akeeagok hardly waited for the other sled to reach the bottom before he launched his, while I, more cowardly slithered down on my own. I half expected to find broken sleds and crushed dogs at the bottom, but nothing serious had happened. The sleds had remained upright, the loads had not shifted and the steamrollered dogs were busy fighting each other.

We sledged for twenty hours, the snow falling heavier all the time. The valley branched and branched again, and we wondered, uneasily, whether our route would lead us to the height of land or end in a steep-cliffed cul-de-sac. After fourteen hours sleep, we found our camp all but buried in snow. The boys still thought it was a great lark, but their fathers were obviously worried. This was not the easy crossing they had envisaged and we were low on food for the dogs.

We climbed the highest mountain in the area to get some idea which valley might be the right one. Again I marvelled at the ease and skill with which they worked their way upwards on the steep snow slopes and across the treacherous scree fields. I panted behind, slipping and scared, and reached the top, exhausted, nearly half an hour after them.

"No good," Akpaleeapik said, sitting at the edge and thoughtfully smoking his pipe.

That was putting it mildly. To begin with, we were sledging up the wrong valley. A few miles further it turned sharply east and disap-

The snow is soft, the scenery magnificent, as the dogs haul with all their might up into a valley on Devon Island

peared between rugged mountains. The only valley stretching nearly due south was a narrow, canyon-like cleft which looked as if it would end in a cliff-girt impasse.

The snow in this valley was deep and soft. To make it even worse it was snowing heavily again. Seeglook and I walked ahead to break a trail and lure on the dogs while the others helped to haul the sleds. Every time we stopped, Akpaleeapik dropped into the snow, contorted by cramps, retching violently, his face a mask of pain. We urged him to camp and rest, but he wouldn't hear of it. On we went, struggling through the snow—on, but fortunately also up. The valley rose more than we had dared to hope. After fifteen hours of toil, we came to its end—a sheer twenty-foot wall of snow flanked by cliffs.

While Akpaleeapik and the boys set up camp, Akeeagok and I began to dig a trench through the snow wall. We all took turns at this work and in five hours we had a narrow and fairly steep, but passable road to the plateau beyond. Then we crawled into our sacks and slept like the dead for ten hours.

A storm was raging outside, but we had no more food for the dogs and Akpaleeapik insisted we continue. On the plateau the storm's full fury hit us, carrying with it such a mass of snow we could sometimes barely see our dogs. Every once in a while we stopped, pored over our maps and then stumbled on, unseeing, through the whirling snow in this winter wonderland gone mad.

Once our sled suddenly picked up speed. We threw ourselves off, held it back with all our strength, and the dogs, alert to the urgency in Akpaleeapik's voice, turned at right angles. When the sled veered and stopped, we were fifteen feet away from a curlicued overhang and a fifty-foot sheer drop.

Worst of all, none of us had a clue where exactly we were. Eskimos have an excellent sense of direction, but when zigzagging through a blinding snow storm in an area they do not know, they can get as lost as anyone else. They do have a fantastic memory for every detail of places they have been to. On a previous trip, I sledged with an Eskimo in Foxe Basin, northern Hudson Bay. We got lost in dense fog. The wind had veered, and we with it, and we travelled all day not knowing where we were or in which direction we were heading. Once the fog lifted a bit and in the distance we could see a small portion of a cliff. The Eskimo, who had been past it before, recognized it instantly, knew where he was and changed course accordingly. But this uncanny ability to imprint upon their minds every configuration along hundreds of miles of arctic coasts, and recognize it years later, did not help us, since neither brother had crossed Devon Island at this place before.

We had hoped to find the beginning of a valley leading from the plateau down to Maxwell Bay, but by the time we found a valley, it was already deep and steep-cliffed, and we sledged on, parallel to it, skirting equally steep-walled side valleys. We reached the plateau's edge after another twenty hours of sledging.

The dogs were just about done for and Akpaleeapik, who had been unable to eat and had trudged through knee-deep snow most of the day, was wracked by pain. Mercifully, we had emerged at a spot where the descent from the mountains to an arm of Maxwell Bay below was feasible. At least that's what the Eskimos said. To me it looked highly dangerous. The ground fell away steeply for one hundred yards or so, levelled out into a bench, fell abruptly another hundred yards and levelled out again, like a long succession of ski jumps. Akpaleeapik and Akeeagok wrapped chains around the sled runners. It had finally stopped snowing and the storm had blown itself out, but in that even, shadowless light I found it difficult to judge the steepness of the slopes.

"You ride?" Akeeagok asked me, a bit sarcastic.

I had been on the verge of saying I'd just as soon get down on my own, but now I said, "Oh sure, I'd be delighted to ride down." The total run, I guessed, was about one thousand yards.

Akpaleeapik whipped the dogs. They whined and tried to go everywhere, except ahead. Apapak, an abject coward at the best of times, got stuck on the highest note of his coloratura register, remembering, no doubt, the bang he got last time it went downhill. Finally Akeeagok came to our help, threw half a dozen dogs down the slope, including the shrilling Apapak, gave our sled a shove and we plunged in a cloud of snow. The heavy sled hurtled down like a falling stone, slowed on the bench, leapt over the next rim and raced again, and we clung to it, blinded by flying snow. It was a wild and exhilarating ride, just the thing after days of tedious trudging through deep, soft snow. The dogs barrelled down the mountain as if all the fiends of hell were after them, Apapak, still yammering, kept on his feet, and we all got safely to the bottom just in time to see Akeeagok take the plunge. He was less lucky. One of his runners caught on a stone, the sled veered, turned over and over while Akeeagok and Seeglook jumped free and came tumbling after.

CHAPTER EIGHT

Now that we were back on sea ice, our fortunes improved. We had not been sledging long, when Akpaleeapik turned to me.

"*Ookpik*" (snowy owl), he said and motioned ahead. As usual I saw nothing. Not only did the Eskimos discover everything first, but even when they pointed things out to me I had no end of trouble seeing them. The only time I ever saw something on my own, was when I discovered a large seal sleeping near the shore. "Akpaleeapik, look! A seal," I said, pleased to show him something for a change. "Good," he said, diffidently. We sledged close to my seal. I could clearly see its head and spindle-shaped body. Any moment now the seal would look up, twist around and disappear into its hole. It never did. It was a rock. Akpaleeapik looked straight ahead, but I could see his shoulders shake with laughter.

Now I couldn't, for the life of me, see that owl. Of course the great arctic owl is nearly pure white and when it sits on snow it doesn't exactly stand out. Still, Akpaleeapik was giving me a running commentary on the owl: ". . . he kill something, he eat, he big man owl," while I was peering desperately ahead trying to discern the white bird in all this whiteness. I saw it, just before it took off on broad silent wings, to settle on a boulder some hundred yards ahead. It had killed a large arctic hare and eaten part of the head. We appropriated the rest for hare stew at night, and as we sledged past the boulder the great owl, its beautiful white plumage delicately barred with brown, glared balefully at us with bright-yellow eyes.

Further down the bay, Akeeagok spotted a seal, stalked it with finesse and his white screen and shot it through the head. The dogs, revitalized by the mere prospect of food, raced off at top speed on the smooth ice.

"*Tiggak*" (a stinker), said Akeeagok, wrinkling his nose when we got off. It was a big old male seal in rut, and he exuded a strong and rather repulsive smell. The dogs didn't mind. We camped nearby, and as soon as the dogs were tethered Akeeagok divided the seal into twenty-nine reasonably equal portions, while the huskies drooled and howled in eager anticipation; they devoured the one hundred and fifty-pound seal in a couple of minutes.

We stopped next day near a ship-shaped island, the steep blunt bow striated, like a layer cake, in narrow bands of chocolate and cream. Now that we had returned to sea ice, it was bear-spotting time again. Akpaleeapik and Akeeagok spent an hour peering patiently through their telescopes and came back with the news that they had seen a bear near the mouth of the bay.

The ice on the bay was perfect for sledging, quite smooth and covered with a thick layer of softly undulating hard snow. The dogs, rested from the rigours of the overland trek, trotted briskly. We sledged another ten miles along the shore of the bay and set up camp on a snow-free stretch of gravel of a raised beach. The brothers climbed a nearby hill and continued their patient scanning of the ice beyond.

A few hours later they returned. "Seven bears," Akeeagok

The boys watch the dogs in Maxwell Bay, off Lancaster Sound, while their fathers look for polar bear from the top of the huge stratified cliff of an island

announced. Five were among the pressure ice out on Lancaster Sound, but two bears were in the bay. It was becoming increasingly hazy and by the time we had readied the sleds, the grey-white pall of a whiteout, caused by the crystallization of moisture in the air, enveloped us in a chilly embrace.

The bear did not see us until we were within a few hundred yards. He was immense and fat, and galloped off, puffing and panting. Akpaleeapik released eight of our dogs and they quickly caught up with the bear. He shooed them off with one mighty swipe of his paw and ran on, but the dogs, yapping and snarling, pressed him hard, nipping at his haunches, and he paused frequently to swat at the pesky pack. When we were within fifty yards, Akpaleeapik dropped off the sled and fired. The bear spun around, then jumped ahead and tumbled out of sight behind a snow ridge. The same instant our remaining sled dogs, eager to join the fray, shot forward, Akpaleeapik was left behind, and Iseechee and I headed for the bear, with nothing more deadly between us than a couple of cameras. We did not see the bear until we were nearly upon him. We should, of course, have jumped off the sled, but poor Iseechee now felt responsible for it and I was so preoccupied with my cameras that it somehow didn't occur to me that to approach a possibly wounded and certainly enraged bear might have unpleasant consequences.

The bullet had merely grazed the bear's neck. He had backed up against the snow ridge and was swatting furiously at the dogs. The moment he saw and smelled us, he charged and the dogs scattered. Iseechee and I raced back towards Akpaleeapik. We could hear a lot of snarling and howling behind us, but we never stopped. Akpaleeapik shot, ran closer and shot again and the bear was dead.

Akpaleeapik was furious. He yelled at both of us, and Iseechee and I felt sheepish and shaky. Akeeagok and Seeglook had caught up with us, Akpaleeapik simmered down and we drove the dogs away from the bear. It was a great male, nearly ten feet long and weighing probably close to a thousand pounds. The brothers walked around the bear, examining its fur and the gunshot wounds, and the dogs lay in the snow around us.

The men were still smoking and gloating over their prize, when Akeeagok suddenly whispered: "Nanook!"

Lumbering out of that white gloom was another bear, heading straight for us. We watched him, mesmerized, as he shuffled along unconcerned, sniffed at a seal hole and came on, hardly a hundred yards away.

Suddenly one of the dogs snarled, the bear stopped, peered ahead, rose on his hind feet and stood fully erect, like a shaggy-furred giant. Our dogs, alerted by our silence and intent staring, spotted the bear and streaked towards him. For one more instant the bear stood, stunned by this sudden onslaught, then dropped to all fours, wheeled and galloped off, with dogs and Eskimos in hot pursuit. The dogs soon caught up with him and Akeeagok, far ahead of the others, shot the bear.

It took most of the night to skin both bears. While we worked, the dogs lay around in a wide expectant circle, drooling and yipping with impatience, and snarling at each other in jealous anger. Slowly they slid closer, eyes gleaming. The men cut off the haunches and loaded each sled with some four hundred pounds of meat, while both boys with whips held the dogs in check. Then, at a word, the dogs jumped forward and threw themselves upon the carcasses with famished ferocity. There was plenty for all, but instead of feasting they spent the first five minutes in a mad fight, each one wanting that pile of meat all to himself. Finally, having to some extent settled who would eat next to whom, they ripped and tore into the carcasses, gulping down meat and guts in frantic haste. Muzzles and heads covered with gore, long fur matted with blood, they soon looked like a ravening pack of hounds from hell.

Only Apapak got nothing. He slunk around, drooling and wagging his tail, trying to steal up unobserved, and get a bit of meat, but the nearest husky would instantly turn on him with a furious flash of teeth.

"How much can the dogs eat?" I asked Akpaleeapik.

"Oh, about ten to fifteen pounds each," he said.

The dogs couldn't stop. Their bellies were bulging, they belched and burped loudly, walked hesitantly away, then hurried back to grab just one more bite. They were so full they could barely move, bloated like balloons, yet they just couldn't keep away from that marvellous pile of meat. Finally we drove them off, to give poor famished Apapak his chance. We sat around and smoked, and Apapak ate as if he hadn't had a meal in weeks and did not expect ever to have another one. He ate more slowly than the huskies, but with methodical determination. Even the Eskimos, used to such sights, seemed fascinated to see that dog expand until I thought he'd bust any moment.

The dogs were lazy after their feast and pulled the sleds slowly and reluctantly. The damp, raw cold crept through our clothes and we sat sleepy and shivering on the rolled-up pelts of the bears.

As they wait for their ration of meat the dogs lick their chops in eager anticipation

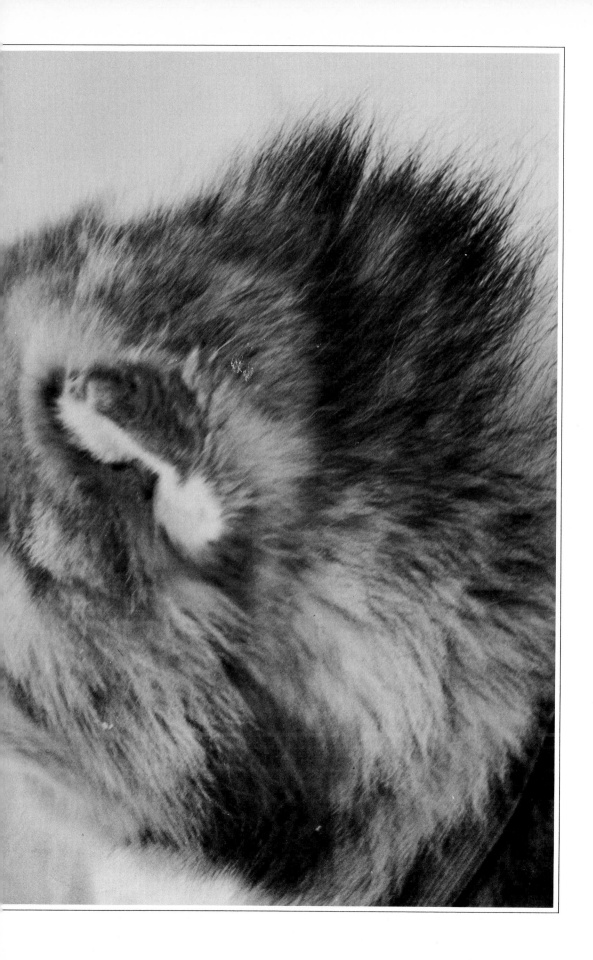

And suddenly, like phantoms out of that all-enveloping whiteness, two more bears appeared, again close and again heading straight towards us. The brothers released all the dogs at once and we ran: first the bears, then a long string of dogs, then Akeeagok—incredibly fast—the two boys, Akpaleeapik and, bringing up the rear, me toting my cameras, sweating, stumbling and swearing. The dogs, gorged with food, showed little enthusiasm for a long chase. Apapak who, perhaps wisely, never had much use for chasing bears, dropped out of the race after fifty yards and many of the huskies, too, began to lag. The bears would, no doubt, have escaped had their path not suddenly been blocked by a wide lead of open water. They could have easily plunged in, swum across and saved themselves on the other side, but for some reason both preferred to stand and face the enemy. Akeeagok shot both bears and they tumbled into the lead. One Akeeagok managed to grab and hold, but the other sank down into the dark icy water.

I was wet with sweat and didn't feel like returning to the sled for an icy ride. I thought I could see the mountains above our camp through the milky haze. It looked like a couple of miles away.

"Camp there?" I asked Akpaleeapik. He raised his eyebrows, which means "yes" in Eskimo (to wrinkle your nose means "no").

"I'll walk," I said.

He looked a trifle surprised.

"Okay," he said.

It was a good ten miles. Akeeagok and the boys were sound asleep when I stumbled up to our tents four hours later. Only Akpaleeapik was awake. He was keeping my supper warm. I wolfed down a gargantuan portion of polar bear stew, until I felt as bloated as the huskies outside. It had again been more than twenty-four hours since our last meal. Then we all slept for thirteen hours. We were reverting to a more ancient mode of life, one dictated by the demands of travel and hunting and not by the regular day and night division of time of more southerly latitudes, or Western man's clock-regulated rhythm of life. For us, extremely long periods of sustained effort were followed by, for white man's standards, abnormally long periods of sleep.

Akeeagok shot another bear next day. The hunters had spotted several bears from their hill, but all were in or near the pressure ice. The bear we followed smelled us early and headed into the worst ice, but Akeeagok followed with some of the dogs for several miles— they brought the bear to bay, and he shot it. We raised another bear, but it turned out to be a female with cubs and, since they are protected, the Eskimos did not follow. This bear had three cubs, an extremely rare occurrence. As a rule, polar bears have twins or, less frequently, one cub.

We returned to camp early. Akpaleeapik was wracked by stomach cramps, and went to bed; Akeeagok was busy repairing torn boots and, for once, they left the feeding of the dogs to the boys. And this ruined our next hunt. The boys blithely chopped up the whole polar bear Akeeagok had brought back and threw it to the dogs. Next day, the huskies, sated and somnolent from this surfeit of food, were not in a working mood. They only wanted to rest and digest.

There was a bear on the smooth bay ice. We got fairly close, Akpaleeapik released some of the dogs, and yelled his wild "Oorooroorooroo!" hunting cry, but the dogs just looked at him as if to say, "Are you nuts?" and ambled off at a leisurely trot. Cursing Iseechee and the bloated dogs with equal venom, Akpaleeapik whipped our remaining dogs into a gallop and managed to catch one of the laggards. He gave him an awful basting and his frantic screams put some spirit into the other dogs. They loped off, fast enough not to be caught by Akpaleeapik, but not fast enough to catch up with the bear and he escaped with ease.

On the way back to camp we came to a wide, partially snow-filled lead. Akpaleeapik was still in a foul mood, and it didn't help when the dogs, instead of jumping, turned abruptly at right angles and, in sudden fright, raced off along the lead, nearly dumping the sled, and us, into the ditch.

Akeeagok's team is in trouble—half his dogs jumped across the lead in Maxwell Bay, some drew back and some fell in

The tangled and twisted traces, covered with frozen slush, have to be unravelled—
a cold and tedious job

It was nearly three weeks now since we had left Grise Fiord and
the bad weather and sudden setback in hunting seemed to have
dampened the brothers' initial enthusiasm for a long stay in the
Maxwell Bay area.

"We go to Resolute," Akpaleeapik said, when we returned to
camp.

Such decisions always caught me by surprise. At first I had
questioned Akpaleeapik and Akeeagok nearly every day, "What will
we do tomorrow?" or, "Where are we going next?" only to get

very vague replies. In part, I think, they did not want to be pinned down to any sort of fixed program. But mainly, they did not know themselves. The life of a hunter is subject to all sorts of unpredictable circumstances: the presence or absence of game animals, the weather and the condition of the hunting terrain. While the trip is planned in its broad outlines, daily decisions are adapted to take maximum advantage of all prevailing circumstances. This gave the impression that everything was done a bit haphazardly and on the spur of the moment, and at first I rather resented the apparent absence of planning. But gradually the pattern began to make sense, and I desisted from the typical white man's impulse to ask, "What will we do tomorrow?" After a while, in fact, it became quite pleasant to shed one's preoccupation with the future, and to live only for the here and now.

We started for Resolute on a dreary day. Wet snow was falling gently as we sledged across Maxwell Bay from Fellfoot Point to Cape William Herschel, intersecting from time to time the tracks we had left during the hunts of the previous days. Slowly the sun struggled through the clouds, for the first time in ten days, and it became quite hot. We were dozing in its warmth, lulled by the gentle swaying of the sled and the monotonous groan of its runners in the snow. Only Akeeagok was alert and it was he who spotted the sleeping bear. He called to us, softly, and we all stopped.

The bear lay a few hundred yards away on an ice block, head on paws, sound asleep. Akpaleeapik and Akeeagok readied their hunting shields and marched off, the older brother leading. When they were sixty yards from the bear, Akpaleeapik knelt, took careful aim, shot—and missed by many feet. The scope on his gun had been knocked out of alignment! The bear who, an instant before had looked like a yellowish rug draped over blue ice, vaulted off the block with lightning swiftness and disappeared into the maze of pressure ice.

Akpaleeapik was livid with rage. It was not just losing the bear; his pride as a hunter was hurt. He slammed the offending rifle down on the sled, when we drove up, missing one of my cameras by inches and effectively dispelling any notions I might have entertained about Eskimos bearing ill fortune with smiling, stoic equanimity. Hardship, yes, plain tough luck, no. Akpaleeapik was blazing mad and while we were brewing tea in cowed and commiserating silence, he cursed bitterly and, every once in a while, kicked the rifle (although, I was amused to note, even in his extreme anger he was careful not to damage it, and later he resighted it with great

91

care). At night we spotted a seal. Akpaleeapik stalked it with even more than usual care and shot it cleanly through the head.

After one sunny day, the clammy cold returned, creeping through our heavy clothes with icy probing fingers. Akpaleeapik was seriously ill. For the last days he had lived solely on tea, cigarettes, and willpower. Sitting all hunched up in front of the great sled in his peaked green parka, he looked like a sick leprechaun. We stopped frequently to make tea and, while we waited for the ice or snow to melt and the water to boil, Akpaleeapik knelt in the lee of the sled, shivering uncontrollably. Neither the cigarettes nor the sodium bicarbonate helped any more. What he needed most was a long rest. But he refused to spare himself and insisted we sledge on.

We reached the extreme southwest corner of Devon Island in the evening. Akpaleeapik pointed to the dark, brooding land ahead.

"Iluvialu," he said. The island of graves.

We were near Beechey Island, the most historic place in the Canadian Arctic.

CHAPTER NINE

Beechey Island had been discovered in the course of Sir William Parry's 1819 expedition in search of the Northwest Passage. One of his officers, Frederick William Beechey, went ashore and reported that the land which at this time formed the western extreme of Devon Island, and which lay on the side of Erebus Bay opposite Cape Riley, was an island. Parry named it Beechey Island. It is not really an island, but a peninsula, connected to Devon Island by a narrow neck of land. But as Beechey Island it became famous, and Beechey Island it has remained.

In 1845 the British Admiralty launched its most determined effort to conquer the Northwest Passage. Sir John Franklin, veteran of many arctic expeditions, was in charge of the venture. He and 128 officers and men sailed from Greenhithe on May 19, 1845, in the ships *Erebus* and *Terror*. On the twenty-sixth of July a Captain Dannett of the whaler *Prince of Wales* met them in Melville Bay. Ten officers from the two expedition ships came aboard. They were in high spirits, confident of success. The vessels parted, and Franklin sailed northwest to disaster and death.

Three years after Franklin's disappearance, the British government dispatched the first of more than forty expeditions that were to search for him during the next decade. Beechey Island became headquarters, rendezvous point and postal station to most of them.

It was Captain H. T. Austin's expedition in 1850 that found the first traces of the missing expedition on Beechey Island: graves, clothes and such masses of equipment that it appeared Franklin had left this island, where he and his men had spent the first winter, in precipitate haste.

From then on, Beechey Island was a busy place. Within weeks of Austin, Sir John Ross arrived with two ships, one of which, the cutter *Mary*, he left at the island. Two years later, Belcher's great expedition lay anchored near its shores, and in 1854 Captain Pullen built Northumberland House, a massive wooden building, amply stocked with food, clothing and coal.

In 1875 Sir Allan Young visited the island and found that polar bears had broken into the depot. He repaired it and left it still well-provisioned and in good order.

But when two men of Sverdrup's expedition sledged down from the *Fram* in 1902, they found the place a shambles. The *Mary* was a wreck, although its wood was still in good condition. Northumberland House had been sacked and plundered.

It was a whaling captain who found out what had happened to depot and ship. He met a party of "unusually well clad" Eskimos in Prince Regent Inlet and they told him happily about the treasure trove their tribe had discovered during a hunting trip to the north on a quite insignificant island. "They were provided with so much tobacco . . . that they declined to barter for the weed from the sailors," the captain reported regretfully.

To most arctic travellers Beechey Island became a nearly obligatory stop, a place of pilgrimage. Roald Amundsen, who first conquered the Northwest Passage in the forty-seven-ton herring boat *Gjoa* and later was the first to reach the South Pole, stopped briefly at Beechey Island; and so did Staff Sergeant Henry Larsen of the RCMP when he made the Northwest Passage in both directions.

The British Admiralty, having spent a fortune on expeditions to find Franklin and his men, abandoned all efforts. But Lady Franklin was determined to ascertain her husband's fate, and all England, gripped by emotional romanticism, was with her. A popular ballad of the day was:

> In Baffin's Bay where the whale-fish blows,
> Is the fate of Franklin—no one knows.
> Ten thousand pounds would I freely give,
> To learn that my husband still did live.
>
> And to bring him back to a land of life,
> Where once again I would be his wife . . .
> I would give all the wealth I ere shall have,
> But I think, alas, he has found a grave.

She spent her fortune to equip one more expedition under Captain Leopold McClintock, with the steam yacht *Fox*. And he did find irrefutable proof of the expedition's fate: a message in a cairn on King William Island, and the bodies of some of the men.

The Eskimos told of ships crushed by ice and of men, poorly equipped to travel in the Arctic, trudging southward, and dying on the trail of hunger, cold, fatigue and scurvy. Franklin may have had a vision of this disaster when, to the question what would happen if he lost his ships, he had replied: "Then I am a gone man." And gone with him were all 128 members of his expedition.

On this lonely island ahead of us, which the Eskimos called "Island of Graves," the first act of the polar tragedy had taken place. The island was now surrounded by a triple barrier of immense pressure ridges, heaved up by tides and the violent currents that swing around Beechey Island.

We made camp close to the outermost ring of upthrust ice. Akpaleeapik went to bed and Akeeagok, his usually so-cheerful face puckered up in worry over his brother, stayed behind to bake bannock and make a broth of seal meat for the invalid.

The boys and I clambered and slithered over the pressure ridges and climbed the steep island slope. We saw a beacon on the highest point of the plateau-like top of the island, a tall mast, set securely in a high mound of stones. At one time, barrels must have been fastened near the mast's top, but they had broken apart and staves lay scattered at its base.

We walked to the northern rim of the plateau, and looked down on Union Bay and Erebus Bay. Clouds were scudding across the sky, fog-like and ragged, a wan sun struggled out, and the light changed from grey to a sulphurous sickly yellow, and then to gloomy grey again as more clouds moved over the sun.

It was Seeglook who spotted the graves, four dark dots near the sea, incredibly lonely in the eerie grey-yellow light. Before I could stop him, he jumped over the edge and glissaded standing on the hard snow, arms waving wildly to keep his balance, struck a spot of soft snow, pitched forward and down he went like a rock, rolling over and over, to disappear at the bottom of the slope in a bank of powdery snow. He emerged, chortling with glee, and watched Iseechee and me slide down, less bravely, on our behinds.

The graves were near the coast, marked by massive slabs of weathered wood. We knelt in the snow to decipher the inscriptions, once burned in, but now standing in black relief:

SACRED
TO THE MEMORY OF
JOHN HARTNER
OF H M
EREBUS

The second read:

SACRED
TO
THE MEMORY OF
JOHN TORRINGTON
WHO DEPARTED
THIS
LIFE JANUARY 18
AD 1846
ON BOARD
H M SHIP TERROR
AGED 20 YEARS

The third inscription was nearly completely effaced. The fourth slab bore no inscription at all. On a lichen-encrusted stone nearby someone had painted in large black letters R.I.P.

We spent a couple of hours searching for the Franklin monument along the west coast of Beechey Island, then turned east and found it on a large shelving peninsula jutting out into Erebus Bay at the foot of a towering cliff. Of Northumberland House only the outline was discernible in the snow, and one corner remained, revealing the massive hewn timbers used in its construction. Near the shore, a boom or mast of the *Mary*, its lower end stuck in a mound of stones, leaned over broken planks and rusted nails and bolts. On the next higher raised beach area stood the monument, a massive white marble slab, laid at a slant on a badly cracked cement base and, at its head, a tall, white, wooden post, surmounted by a knob, looking rather like an old-fashioned country gate post.

Ironically, it was the man leading the last official expedition in search of Franklin and his men, who had brought along their tombstone. Originally the stone had been entrusted by Lady Franklin to Lieutenant H. J. Hartstene, an American who was setting out to find another missing expedition, that of Dr. Elisha Kent Kane. He was unable to reach Beechey Island and left the stone at Disco, in Greenland. There Captain Leopold McClintock picked it up when he passed in the *Fox* on his way to determine the fate of Sir John Franklin.

In the strange fulvous twilight, we read the inscription on the polished marble slab:

TO THE MEMORY OF FRANKLIN, CROZIER, FITZJAMES AND ALL THEIR GALLANT BROTHER OFFICERS AND FAITHFUL COMPANIONS WHO SUFFERED AND PERISHED IN THE CAUSE OF SCIENCE AND IN THE SERVICE OF THEIR COUNTRY THIS TABLET IS ERECTED NEAR THE SPOT WHERE THEY PASSED THEIR FIRST ARCTIC WINTER AND WHENCE THEY

ISSUED FORTH TO CONQUER DIFFICULTIES OR TO DIE. IT COMMEMORATES THE GRIEF OF THEIR ADMIRING COUNTRYMEN AND FRIENDS AND THE ANGUISH, SUBDUED BY FAITH, BY HER WHO HAS LOST IN THE HEROIC LEADER OF THE EXPEDITION, THE MOST DEVOTED AND AFFECTIONATE OF HUSBANDS.

AND SO HE BROUGHT THEM UNTO HEAVEN
WHERE THEY WOULD BE— 1855.

THIS STONE HAS BEEN ENTRUSTED AND IS AFFIXED IN ITS PLACE BY THE OFFICERS AND CREW OF THE AMERICAN EXPEDITION COMMANDED BY LT. H. J. HARTSTENE IN THE SEARCH OF DR. KANE AND HIS COMPANIONS.

Below this, an inscription read: "This tablet having been left at Disco by the American expedition which was unable to reach Beechey Island in 1855 was put on board the discovery yacht *Fox* and is now set up here by Capt. McClintock, R.N., commanding the final expedition of search for ascertaining the fate of Sir John Franklin and his companions."

A small marble tablet, affixed to the wooden post, was the monument to yet another man who died in this bleak region:

IN MEMORY OF LIEUT. BELLOT OF THE FRENCH NAVY WHO LOST HIS LIFE WHILE NOBLY AIDING IN THE SEARCH FOR SIR JOHN FRANKLIN, IN THE WELLINGTON CHANNEL, WHERE HE WAS DROWNED ON THE 1ST OF AUGUST 1853. THIS TABLET, TO RECORD THE SAD EVENT, WAS ERECTED BY HIS FRIEND JOHN BARROW, A.D. 1854.

We began the long walk back to camp. Seeglook, still chipper after a twenty-six-hour day, was running ahead and jumping into any suitable snowdrift. We found a valley leading to the plateau and climbed up, Seeglook (pretending to be a bear) running on all fours and grunting loudly, Iseechee, rather tired, behind and I trailing, slow and thoughtful. Halfway up the slope I stopped to rest. Below were the graves, incredibly lonely, four dark spots in a vastness of snow and rock, standing out clearly in the slanting rays of a pale yellow sun flanked by even paler mock suns.

During the last few miles I rather looked forward to a good long sleep, but by the time I reached the tents the Eskimos had begun to break camp. There was only time to drink a lot of tea, eat some of Akeeagok's freshly baked bannock with little chunks of frozen seal meat, and we were off again. Akpaleeapik was eager to reach Resolute as quickly as possible. We camped in the middle of Wellington Channel and the next day drove at a good clip over smooth ice to the coast of Cornwallis Island. The sun was dazzling, the snow aglitter, it was warm and pleasant. Seals were lying everywhere near their breathing-holes, some so lazy they would let us come to within thirty yards with our sleds. Near Cape Dungeness, we dug a deep hole into a snowdrift, buried most of our belongings and rushed with light sleds to Resolute, following a well-travelled trail. When we came in sight of the houses, the dogs burst into wild gallop, we skimmed across ice and snow and were greeted by a welcoming chorus of howls from several tethered dog teams.

CHAPTER TEN

Within minutes of our arrival in Resolute Bay we seemed to be surrounded by half the village's population. Children came running to see us. Women rushed out of the houses, and men hurried down to the ice, pulling on parkas as they ran. It was Saturday afternoon and nearly everyone was home from work. Akpaleeapik and Akeeagok shook hands all around while I stood by, feeling very much odd man out. We walked up to a house and settled in its large kitchen, strewn with clothes and magazines.

After a while an Eskimo, speaking perfect English, suddenly turned to me and asked: "Do you know anyone here?"

"I know the administrator," I said.

"He's away. But I'll phone the police from the house next door. They will find you a place to stay." He left and was back in a few minutes.

"I speak to the police. You go to the other house. The police will call you back there right away."

I went and waited. The Eskimo woman made me a cup of tea and the children stared at me in wide-eyed wonder. Suddenly the telephone jangled. I picked it up.

"What are you doing there?" asked a stern voice, without further preamble.

"Right now I was waiting for you to call me," I said, a bit annoyed.

"You must not bother the Eskimos," the voice warned. "You are not allowed into the village."

"Look," I said, now quite angry, "I'm not bothering anyone. I just got here and I am looking for a place to stay."

"What do you mean 'you just got there'?" the voice asked. "Where did you come from?"

"From Grise Fiord," I said.

There was a long pause. Then the voice declared firmly: "That

Polar bear skins hang like washing in Resolute Bay, on Cornwallis Island

In the school at Resolute the children have made cutouts and pasted them on white paper, showing how their fathers hunt seal and polar bear

is impossible! There hasn't been a plane in from Grise Fiord in weeks."

"I didn't come by plane," I tried to explain. "I came by dogteam."

"Oh, really?" The voice sounded sarcastic. "Who are you anyway?"

This gave me a chance to tell my story and to convince the Mountie that I was a bona fide dogteam traveller, tired and badly in need of a bath. He said he'd call me back and hung up. A few minutes later the phone rang again.

"This is Jim MacDiarmid," another voice introduced itself. "I'm the teacher here and right now also acting administrator. Come up to my place, you can stay here."

An Eskimo boy showed me the way and Jim met me at the door. "Come in and make yourself at home," he said hospitably, but with a startled glance, and flinching a bit. I knew why when I had a look in the mirror. My cheeks, a narrow strip of brow and my nose were a deep brick red, the lips cracked and nearly black, and the chin covered with a bristly beard. The whole was framing two enormous, dirty-white eye sockets—the area covered by the goggles. I looked like a rather revolting leprous owl.

At night several visitors came, among them the suspicious Mountie. "I'm sorry I gave you such a rude reception," he apologized. "But when the Eskimo phoned and said there was a white photographer hanging about the village I thought it was one of the men from the base, and they are not supposed to be there."

Another visitor was Dick Kruse. He used to work as clerk for the Hudson's Bay Company and I had met him on previous trips to the North.

"Did you see any muskoxen?" he asked.

"No," I said. "But you should be able to see them here. A friend of mine saw a herd at Trafalgar Lake a couple of years ago. And that is only about fifteen miles from Resolute Bay."

"You think they are still there?" Dick asked.

"Probably," I said, quite innocently and not realizing what I was letting myself in for. "If they have sufficient food, muskoxen don't move around much."

"Let's go there tomorrow," said Dick, a great believer in snap decisions. Before I could object that I had travelled plenty, thank you, and would now like to live at leisure, Dick was at the phone, talked rapidly to an Eskimo friend, and hung up five minutes later, thoroughly satisfied.

"It's all fixed," he said. "We'll leave tomorrow morning with

A little boy concentrates on his work at the Resolute Bay school

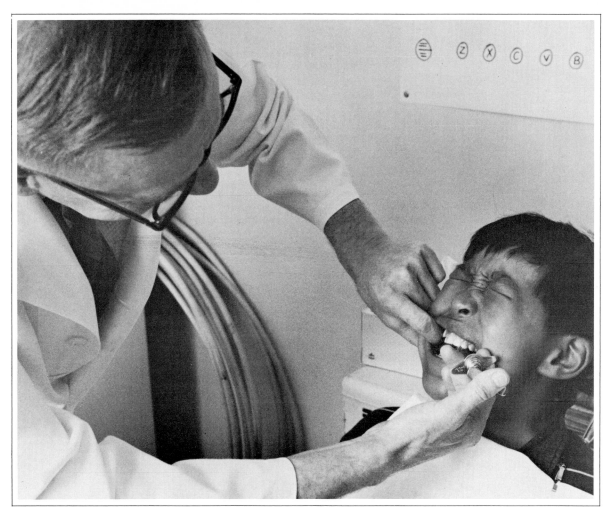

A dentist examines and repairs the children's teeth at the school in Resolute Bay—
his efforts elicit an apprehensive look and a grimace of pain

three skidoos. The Eskimos know where Trafalgar Lake is. It'll
cost you ten bucks each."

We talked until 3 A.M. and then went to bed. But I couldn't
sleep. The room seemed insufferably warm and the bed too soft.
I tossed and turned and toyed with the idea of getting my sleeping
bag and bedding down in the snow on Jim's porch.

It was cold, sunny and very windy as we left, the Eskimos driving
the skidoos, and the kabloonas riding on sleds behind, hanging
on for dear life. We followed the coast of Cornwallis Island, travelling
fast on smooth sea ice, and then cut inland to Trafalgar Lake. No
muskoxen. Dick looked at me accusingly.

"Where are your muskoxen?" he asked

"They were here three years ago," I said defensively.

"But where are they now?" Dick wanted to know. He seemed to take it for granted that I must be au courant with all the muskoxen's movements in the interim.

"No idea," I said. "Let's try the next valley."

We zoomed up a long slope—and down in the valley were four muskoxen. They took off immediately, but one of the Eskimos jettisoned his sled and passenger and raced after them. As he came close, three muskoxen stopped in an abrupt volte-face, while the fourth, a large female, rushed on in a cloud of billowing snow.

We drove to within a respectful fifty yards and looked at our muskoxen: a great bull with magnificent horns, meeting on his brow in a massive, grooved boss, sweeping down on either side of his head in yellowish curves and tilting up into sharp, polished, dark-brown tips; a cow, her horns more slender than those of the bull but not less sharp; and a young animal. Their long fur, like an immense wraparound sporran, hung nearly to the ground.

In the happy days before man, the muskox's main enemy was the wolf, and against him the muskox evolved an efficient form of defence, the "hedgehog formation." When wolves attack, the muskoxen of a herd crowd together in a circle or semicircle, with calves and immature animals in the centre, their sharp, curved horns facing the enemy. Should an incautious wolf come too close, the nearest muskox rushes out, tries to gore and trample him and then returns to the protective circle of the herd. This stratagem worked fine as long as the muskoxen had only to deal with lupine attackers. Against men and guns it was suicidal. Muskoxen were slaughtered by the tens of thousands, until the pitiful remnant received full protection in Canada in 1917. Since then, the muskox has made a slow but steady comeback and now there are again about ten thousand muskoxen in Canada.

I got my cameras ready and walked close to our three muskoxen. The bull advanced a couple of steps, the cow and the young animal hid behind him. At forty feet the bull began to paw the snow and to rub his head against the foreleg, two sure signs of extreme annoyance in muskoxen. Sometimes they precede a charge. I looked back. The others were watching my progress with somewhat apprehensive interest. One of the Eskimos waved a cautioning hand. I took some pictures and ventured a few steps closer. The bull rubbed his head again and took another step forward. He looked majestic and somehow prehistoric. In a way he was. During the latter part of the Pleistocene the muskox roamed large areas of Europe and America in the company of sabre-toothed tigers, mastodons and mammoths. They all died out, but the muskox remained, shaggy, craggy and archaic, braving the elements of his arctic realm. The bull took another slow, deliberate step forward and I began to back up.

I still wanted a good set of close-up pictures. I talked it over with the Eskimos and they slowly drove the skidoos closer, until they were only twenty-five yards from the muskoxen.

On a vast white plain, thirty miles from Resolute Bay, we came upon three musk-oxen: a bull, a cow, and a young animal

As we came closer, the three muskoxen did their best to try and form a defensive circle

The lead bull, looking powerful and somehow archaic, like an animal from an age long past, advances a few steps

Alarmed by the sudden noise of the skidoos, the three muskoxen gallop away, long fur flying, through clouds of powdery snow

"If the bull attacks, we'll try to cut him off," one of them said. "But you better run fast or he'll skewer you." In Norway, I remembered, a provoked muskox (they were introduced there from Greenland after World War II) had gored and killed a man. It was not a cheering thought.

I started another slow advance. The bull stared at me with bloodshot eyes. When he pawed the snow and snorted, I stood still and waited. When he calmed down, I advanced. At twenty-five feet, the Eskimos behind me called a warning. I stopped, knelt in the snow and finished slowly the film in each camera. The gleaming horns looked enormous in the viewfinder. My hands were sweating despite the cold. I inched back and changed films.

"You wait here," the Eskimos said. They drove off and circled around the three muskoxen who, for a while, tried valiantly to face all their enemies at once, turning and trampling back and forth in apparent indecision. Suddenly they broke formation and rushed towards me through the deep soft snow. Their long hair waved in the wind, like an enormous, dark, fringed blanket.

They paid no attention to me. Intent only on getting away from the machines, they galloped past, nearly envelopped in clouds of powdery snow, and disappeared over the crest of the nearest ridge.

We drove back inland to Resolute, over high rolling hills, down into deep valleys and up again, the Eskimos racing their skidoos against each other and having a marvellous time. They did lose their passengers from time to time, when the sleds overturned, but the snow was soft and once they were aware that one of us was no longer with them, all turned back in haste to pick the straggler up.

It stormed for the next three days. I enjoyed the comforts of Jim's hospitable home, took pictures in the school and of the dentist who had come from Edmonton to fix the children's teeth. While I winced and developed sympathetic aches in every tooth, most of the kids endured the drilling or pulling with amazing stoicism. The last patient was the janitor's little girl, a tiny, moon-faced, serious-eyed four-year-old. Two of her teeth were damaged and had to be pulled.

"Tell her it will hurt a bit," the dentist told the father. This palliative phrase, I knew from sad experience, really means "it will hurt like hell," and I cringed in anticipative sympathy. The janitor spoke to the little girl and she looked with her big dark eyes at the man in the white coat, her face completely expressionless.

The first tooth came out. The little girl did not cry or flinch. She sat immobile in the big chair and looked fixedly at the dentist.

"Did it hurt?" he asked.

"Yes," she said.

"We have to pull one more." the dentist said, apologetically. When that was interpreted, the little girl obediently opened her mouth wide, looking all the time at the dentist with the same serious intentness. Out came the second tooth. She did not blink an eye. She just sat there watching the dentist's every move

"It's all over," he said and patted her. She climbed off the chair, got a candy, mumbled a little "thanks," and wandered off at her father's hand, as solemnly reflective as she had come.

The third evening the storm started to falter and Akpaleeapik came to visit.

"We go tomorrow," he said. He looked fine. The hard, haggard lines in his face had vanished and he seemed relaxed and content.

"I eat lots of caribou," he said. "Drink little bit beer. Nurse give me tablets. Now everything okay."

In the evening we went to the movie in the community hall. The place was packed with Eskimos, mainly children who chased each other over, under and around the seats. The film, *Ship of Fools*, started a bit jerkily and out-of-focus, but that was soon adjusted. The volume was deafening, but even at that it was at times drowned out by the screams of the kids. They had a glorious time playing hide and seek in the semi-darkness. No one understood the film, but it moved, it was very noisy, it was a big family party and everybody enjoyed himself immensely.

We left early next day in fine weather. The dogs were rested and ran with a will. The sleds were light and my Eskimos in high good humour. We dug up our cache and reloaded the sleds with the usual meticulous attention to detail and with every box in precisely the same place as during the entire preceding trip. We sledged on past the shore of Cornwallis Island, low, rolling and monotonous after the dramatic cliffs of Devon and Ellesmere Islands. The seals were sleeping soundly on the ice as if they didn't have an enemy in the world. They were moulting and that makes them rather lethargic. Since anything dark on the white expanse of snow and ice excited the dogs' attention and enthusiasm, we proceeded in an erratic zigzag course from seal to seal. We nearly ran on top of one, it dived an instant before the dogs grabbed it. The next one paid for its somnolence with its life. Akpaleeapik dropped off the sled when we were thirty yards away and shot the seal through the head.

We camped below Cape Hotham, where the island rock had been sharply tilted into an immense scalene triangle. Akpaleeapik pro-

Heavy ground drift near Cornwallis Island's Cape Hotham slowly buries our sleds, our tents and our dogs

duced a big burlap bag. "Caribou meat," he said happily. "My friends give it to me. Good for my stomach." I cooked a huge pot of it. Without salt!

I dreamt at night I was flying, higher, ever higher, right into cold, wet clouds. The wind shrieked about me and my face froze in the icy mist. I awoke with a start. The tent was flapping wildly. It had torn out from underneath the boxes and I was half buried in snow. I got up in a rush, tried to weigh down the tent flaps and to get the snow off my sleeping bag before it melted. Akpaleeapik dressed quickly and went outside to build a protective snow wall around our tent. The dogs were already covered by snow and our sleds were part of a rapidly growing drift. We slept and ate all day, while the storm whistled about the tent in icy blasts. It was the first day of June.

The storm blew itself out during the next night and was followed by frigid fog. We sledged northward on Wellington Channel, along the east coast of Cornwallis Island. It was cold, clammy and unpleasant. But every once in a while we saw flocks of birds skimming past us through the murk—ducks, and jaegers, and guillemots—off to their summer breeding grounds even further north. I shivered on the sled. Summer seemed a long way off.

Curled up tightly, one of our sled dogs sleeps, oblivious to the drifting snow which will slowly cover him

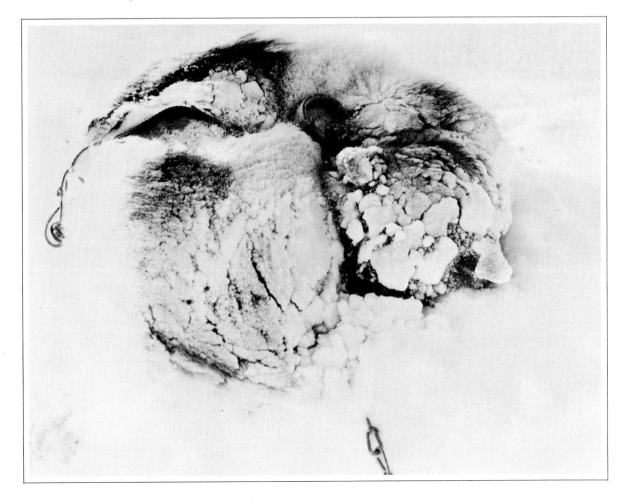

CHAPTER ELEVEN

After sledging for three days through the dismal grey-white of fog and drifting snow, we emerged exactly where Akpaleeapik had said we would, Dragleybeck Inlet on northwestern Devon Island.

"Tomorrow we hunt caribou," Akpaleeapik said. "Akeeagok goes, and you and Iseechee." Quite recovered now, Akpaleeapik was his usual decisive self. When I awoke next morning, Akpaleeapik was gone. He returned while I was making breakfast. "Three caribou, one seal," he announced. The brothers had spotted them from a hill near camp.

Akeeagok stalked and shot the seal. Then we drove north into Baring Bay. The land looked inhospitably desolate—wide pebbly beaches, intersected by high gravel ridges, rising further inland to low rolling hills.

We left Iseechee to guard the dogs and walked inland, Akeeagok leading the way through the ridge-pleated area near shore and from there up into a shallow valley. After a couple of miles Akeeagok cautiously peered over the valley's rim. Three caribou were peacefully browsing lichen on the gently sloping side of a hill ahead of us.

They were Peary caribou, the caribou subspecies of the high arctic regions. Unlike the large herds of Barren Ground caribou, most of whom make annually an immense migration from the northern forest belt over the tundra, and back to the taiga again in fall, the Peary caribou do not wander widely. They are smaller than their mainland cousins, nearly pure white, with a grey-brown saddle.

The three caribou in front of us were standing on a wide plain. There was no rock or ridge that would have permitted Akeeagok to sneak up on them unobserved.

"You walk behind me like that," he instructed, bending at right angles.

"I walk like this," he stood upright, his head bent forward. "Maybe caribou think we caribou. I front, you back."

Could I, in my capacity as the rear end of a caribou, still carry my cameras, I asked.

"Oh yes," Akeeagok assured me. "Caribou don't see so good."

This, I felt, had to be true, because we did not make a very convincing caribou, Akeeagok with his gun and binoculars and I festooned with cameras. At least we both wore white parkas.

We emerged from our hiding place and walked across the plain straight towards the myopic and unsuspecting animals. When we came to within a hundred and fifty yards, they stopped browsing and stared curiously at us. Akeeagok reassured them with a few throaty caribou grunts. "Don't stop!" he whispered to me, worried lest I tarry to take a picture and our caribou act would split into two totally unconvincing halves.

At a hundred yards the caribou were clearly upset. Something, they seemed to realize, was distinctly odd about this approaching creature. Akeeagok stopped. "Turn with me," he whispered. He turned slowly, grunting all the time, and I turned with him, my head in the small of his back, intent not to botch the rearend part of the performance. Seeing us thus, in profile, seemed to ease the caribou's worry. Akeeagok grunted. The caribou walked back and forth, torn between curiosity and fear. Then they started to come toward us. Every time they halted, Akeeagok grunted and we advanced a few steps. I felt sorry for the curious caribou, marching so trustingly towards their doom. In this isolated area, where they are rarely hunted, their main enemy must be the arctic wolf.

And a wolf we were not, that much they could see. Since Akeeagok grunted so convincingly, we must be a caribou; a peculiar caribou but a caribou nevertheless. They walked closer, peering intently at us. They were now well within shooting range, but Akeeagok continued to grunt and call. Like most Eskimo hunters, he had a nearly intuitive knowledge of what the game animal would do next. He sensed the crucial instant when caution and fear began to outweigh curiosity, and in that moment he shot two of the caribou. The third broke into a frantic gangly gallop, then changed into a magnificent long-strided pacing gait, circled and began to come back. Akeeagok showed no interest. "Akpaleeapik say two caribou enough," he explained.

Facing page:
Akeeagok has shot a small, nearly white Peary caribou and carries it across gravel ridges to the coast of northwestern Devon Island

Iseechee, who had watched us from a ridge, came tearing up with the sled. We loaded the caribou, stopped to pick up the seal and drove back to camp. I fried caribou liver with thin strips of backfat while the men packed the sleds so we could leave right after lunch. We had a big meal and then sledged south for a couple of miles, until we reached a wide river valley. Here we would begin our second crossing of Devon Island to regain Jones Sound. But first Akpaleeapik wanted to show me something.

We left the sleds in charge of the boys and walked along a pebble beach, strewn with convoluted marine whelk shells, to the river delta. After a mile, Akpaleeapik pointed ahead.

On a gravel bank, between the frozen river arms, stood a shiny bright-yellow skidoo, looking extremely lonely and forlorn. We walked over, Akeeagok twisted levers and yanked at the starting cord, but this only produced a defiant chortle.

Two men from Grise Fiord, Akpaleeapik explained, had gone to Resolute by dogteam. One of them bought the skidoo and drove it proudly back home, until it passed out on this gravel bank. He would have been in desperate straits had not the other man, driving the dogteam, caught up with him. They abandoned the recalcitrant machine and returned to Grise Fiord under dog power.

"Is he just leaving the machine?" I asked.

"Oh no, he'll come back some day and fix it and drive it home," Akpaleeapik said. "But we must put the skidoo some other place. When the snow melts and the river is in spate it might wash over this bank."

We walked back to get a sled. The boys had made tea and we had mugfuls of it—I hot, the Eskimos lukewarm. They always threw handfuls of snow into their tea to cool it off, even on quite cold days, partly because this way they could drink their tea more quickly and were usually finished with their second mug while I was still scalding my lips on the first, but partly also because hot tea made them sweat. If one of them did drink it hot, a sheen of perspiration quickly spread over his face. While I was barely thawing they were usually already too warm.

I used to admire and envy their ability to withstand cold. One day, during our first crossing of Devon Island, Iseechee pulled the zipper of his parka apart. To get the tab down, so the zipper could be properly closed again, all the little links had to be pressed into each other, a fiddly job at any time and absolutely beastly in subzero cold and wind. But Akpaleeapik repaired the zipper, patiently and methodically and in half an hour the job was done. He clapped his

116

Tea break near the coast of Devon Island

hands a couple of times, pulled on his mitts and five minutes later, when he passed me a cigarette, his hands were perfectly warm again. Of course they thought it riotously funny when I, having taken off my mittens for a few minutes to photograph, would hop about like an hysteric ape, trying desperately to get some life back into numbed hands and frozen fingertips.

We were drinking our tea, talking and smoking when suddenly Akpaleeapik straightened up. "Nanook!" he said. Trotting across the inlet, not three hundred yards away, were two polar bears.

We dumped the loads off the sleds and raced after the bears. The ice was smooth, the dogs rested; the bears did not have a chance, unless they could gain land before the hunters reached them. As soon as they saw us they galloped towards shore. Akpaleeapik released six dogs and they streaked after the bears, yapping with excitement. But the bears had only one idea in mind: to reach land. There indeed, they would have been safe, because we could not follow them over the wide patches of bare rock and gravel with our sleds. Akpaleeapik shouted and released all his dogs, and Akeeagok behind us also let loose his entire team. The bears were two hundred yards from shore. But now twenty-nine dogs were pressing in from all sides, snarling and howling, dashing in to attack and darting back when the bears turned on them in fury.

Apapak, as usual, kept well out of the fray. He was as scared of his team mates as of the bears and had no intention of getting mixed up with either if he could possibly help it. He chose what he considered a safe place and watched the action with interest. Unfortunately this happened to be a spot exactly between the beleaguered bears and the shore. When the bears saw the hunters approach they suddenly broke through the circle of yapping huskies and galloped towards Apapak. In his frantic haste to get out of the way, Apapak stumbled, then ran, but the bears were already so close one of them stepped on Apapak's trailing trace. He let out a piercing shriek of anguish, but in the same instant the bears, with huskies snapping at their haunches, turned again and Apapak was safe. Akpaleeapik had now caught up with the bears and shot both of them at close range.

The men skinned the bears, cut one up to serve as dog food on our trip across Devon Island, and turned the dogs loose on the second carcass. Blood-smeared and bloated, they were an evil-looking bunch, as we drove back to where we had so abruptly abandoned our tea and our equipment. We set up the tents on a dry gravel ridge, and hauled the skidoo to high ground before we went to bed.

It was hot and humid when I awoke next day, the first really warm day of our trip. Land and ice lay shrouded in dense grey fog. It was stuffy in the tent, and hundreds of tiny black spiders crawled on its white walls or dangled by silken threads from its roof. The warmth must have lured them forth from their winter quarters amongst the pebbles of the ridge. Akpaleeapik and Akeeagok did not seem to mind them, but the boys were terrified of the spiders. Iseechee was still sleeping, or pretending to sleep, when I boiled bear meat for breakfast. Judging breakfast to be ready, Iseechee opened his eyes and saw two spiders hover an inch above his face. For an instant he froze with fear then, with a nervous giggle, rolled away from underneath the spiders with such alacrity, he nearly upset the burning stove and the boiling meat. Seeglook, usually afraid of nothing, was also scared of the little spiders.

It was amazing to see the change wrought by one day of warm weather. The area of snow-free land had nearly doubled since we had gone to bed. The snow, so hard before, had suddenly turned soft and mushy. We broke camp in haste and headed inland, zig-zagging through a maze of bare gravel ridges, keeping to the snow-filled troughs between them.

As we sledged higher in the river valley the grey fog slowly changed into a luminous golden haze, suddenly the sun broke through, and the snow-covered land shone in dazzling brilliance. It was marvellous to travel in the warm sun. Akpaleeapik sat in his usual place at the front of the sled, keeping up a nearly continuous gutteral chant of orders to his dogs: "Woie! Woie!"—right; "Aghe! Aghe!"—left; or "Aie! Aie!"—go! go!, by way of encouragement. When a dog did not obey his orders, or if he saw by a slack trace that one was not pulling his share, he flicked the thirty-foot whip and hit the sinner with deadly accuracy. This was followed by an instant, sharp yelp of pain and a lunge forward. The other huskies, with a sort of collective twinge of fear—"this might have been meant for me"—joined in a brief gallop and then all returned to their steady trot.

One of the dogs' daily dilemmas was that their natural inclination to squat in peace while defecating was thwarted by the utter impossibility of doing so while pulling, at the same time, a sled. To make matters worse, they knew from bitter experience with the whip that they must go about their business well aside from the following sled. On a cold day, warm excrement freezes instantly to the sled runners, spoiling effectively their smooth gliding surfaces. An Eskimo who has spent half an hour or more carefully icing his runners, is not amused when one of his dogs' *petits accidents* gets stuck to them. For a dog to drop a turd in front of the sled is therefore a cardinal canine sin no Eskimo driver will let pass unpunished. So a dog, urged by nature, had to jump first over the traces of the other dogs, then squat and run to one side of the sled in a rather pathetic hop-and-drop manner, looking all the while intensely worried, because his dragging trace might get run over by the sled and that, he knew, might earn him a beating. Finally, mission accomplished, the relieved dog would skip eagerly back across the other dogs' traces to assume his usual place among his team mates.

After eight hours we reached the height of land. Below us lay a snow-covered lake and from it another valley stretched northeast towards Viks Fiord. Sverdrup had discovered and named this fiord, but the area did not impress him favourably: "A more barren land none of us had seen before—sand, grit, and stones wherever we we went; not the sign of a plant was to be seen, not the track of an animal."

He must have been unlucky, because we saw plenty of tracks. Our route followed the most convenient crossing of Devon Island from the Wellington Channel to the Jones Sound area, and not only was it regularly used by the Grise Fiord Eskimos, but also by polar bears. We saw fairly fresh tracks of eight bears, most of them going, like us, down to Viks Fiord.

During the day it grew intensely hot. The sleds dragged through the wet snow, the dogs panted along listlessly, and we shed our parkas. Near Viks Fiord the sleds began to break through the snow. We jumped off to push and sank up to our hips into slush. Soon we were soaking wet. In some places, melt water was already gushing over the river ice. We ran and pushed and pulled the sled, stepping into hidden holes, floundering in a mire of waterlogged snow. It had taken us twelve hours to cross the island. It took us another five hours for the last three miles to the high gravel ridge at the head of Viks Fiord, sloshing and slipping through the frigid slush.

We set up camp on the ridge, and spread our soaked clothes and boots on the warm pebbles to dry out.

"Sometime there are muskoxen here," Akpaleeapik said. "You want to look?" I was dead tired after that last long haul through the wet snow and not very keen to get my other pair of boots wet. But I had told Akpaleeapik that I was anxious to get more muskox pictures and now he conscientiously remembered it. I agreed, with what I hoped sounded like joyous enthusiasm.

We walked up a small valley, keeping to the side which had been in shade most of the day and where the snow was still fairly hard. The valley made a sharp bend and Akpaleeapik, who walked ahead, stopped.

"Oomingmak" (muskox), he said. It is a nice descriptive name for the shaggy animal. It means "the bearded one."

Facing page:
After crossing Jones Sound we reach again the majestic cliffs of Ellesmere Island

I looked hard and, as usual, could see nothing. Just a mass of rocks a hundred yards ahead. Akpaleeapik turned to Iseechee, gave him some instructions, and he trotted back towards camp. I thought I had heard the word "axe."

"You want an axe?" I asked, puzzled.

"Yes," Akpaleeapik said. "Cut off oomingmak's head," and then, when I looked rather stupid, he added with a laugh: "Oomingmak dead!"

It was a large muskox cow, half buried in the snow. I asked Akpaleeapik what had killed her. He examined the animal carefully.

"Very old," he said. "Maybe many muskox walk up this valley, old cow get stuck in soft snow, stay behind and die."

We sat on the corpse, frozen hard as rock, and smoked and talked. Eskimo is an exceedingly difficult language, full of infixes, prefixes and suffixes for the uninitiated to stumble over. I had, during my trips to the North acquired a fairly good vocabulary, but my notions of grammar were still extremely vague. Akpaleeapik and Akeeagok talked to me in a simplified form of their language, a sort of pidgin Eskimo to which they considerately admixed every English word they knew.

Iseechee came back with the hatchet and Akpaleeapik skilfully chopped off part of the skull with boss and horns. The toggles of the dog harnesses, I had noticed, were carved out of the keratinous sheaths of muskox horns.

The weather had changed, with startling abruptness, to warm, and it changed with equal abruptness back to cold. It was still sunny next day but an icy wind whistled down the narrow fiord. It was ideal sledging weather and the surface, too, was excellent. The previous day's slush-and-water was now smoothly glazed and frozen. The dogs galloped along eagerly, and the sleds, pushed by a strong wind, slithered and clattered over snow and ice. By noon we were near the end of Viks Fiord and made tea below the sheer, thousand-foot, dun-coloured cliffs on the north shore.

Since travelling conditions were perfect, I asked Akpaleeapik if we could make a detour to St. Helena Island, a day's trip away.

"No," he said. "It is impossible. There is open water around the island." He pointed to the north. In the distance a grey-black pall seemed to hover above the ice, vapour rising into the cold air from a large extent of open water. In the Arctic one can also see the reflection of open water a great distance away. Earlier, during our trip, Akpaleeapik had pointed out a lead-coloured cloud far above Lancaster Sound. That was the reflection upon the sky of the sea's dark colour. Sailors used to call it "water sky," as opposed to "iceblink," the sulphurous glare in the sky that indicates extensive icefields.

"Why do you want to go to St. Helena Island?" Akapaleeapik asked.

"Have you been there?" I asked in return.

"Yes," he said, "once in summer."

"Did you see little stone houses?" I asked eagerly. He looked mystified.

"What sort of houses? I don't see any houses."

"Houses for ducks," I said, and then hastened to explain, since Akpaleeapik obviously was thinking that I was pulling his leg.

Sverdrup had visited St. Helena Island in 1901 by boat. He found it a "very interesting little limestone island" where "the tooth of time had eroded the rocks and formed fantastic vaults and grottoes, and adjoining these were long rows of pillars, sometimes standing alone, sometimes framed in deep niches."[1] Thousands of guillemots and eider ducks were nesting on the island.

The men found several "tent rings," stones laid in a circle and used once to weigh down the bottoms of tents, an indication that, centuries before, Eskimos had camped on the island. But what really amazed Sverdrup and his companions was the discovery of little stone houses, structures with which they were familiar from their native Norway.

"As far as I could understand, they [the Eskimos] had even built nests for the ducks of the same construction that is in vogue to this day up in Nordland [Norway]. At all events, we came across a number of very small stone houses. Certainly I have never heard that the Eskimos were in the habit of protecting the birds in this fashion; but everything indicated that we were the first civilized people to visit the spot."

His surprise was understandable. In northern Norway, people along the coast have built, since time immemorial, little stone houses as shelters for eider ducks, whose valuable down they collect. The Vikings introduced the idea to Iceland (where they are used to this day), and later built similar shelters near their settlements in Greenland. And now Sverdrup saw identical little stone houses for ducks on an isolated little island far from Greenland, near the western extremity of Jones Sound.

The reports of these little stone houses created quite a stir in scientific circles. The duck shelters could not be of Eskimo origin, since Eskimos have never been known to build them. And the

[1]From Otto Sverdrup, *New Land,* translated by Ethel Harriet Hearn, 2 vols. (London: Longmans, Green & Company, 1904).

farthest north the Vikings are known to have travelled is Melville Bay, northwestern Greenland, more than six hundred miles from St. Helena Island. Some scientists, notably Vilhjalmur Stefansson, saw in these duck shelters on St. Helena Island proof that the Vikings travelled not only west to Baffin Island, and south to Labrador and Newfoundland, but that they also penetrated far west in the high Arctic. Their reasoning was simple: the duck shelters on St. Helena Island are typical Viking constructions, consequently they must have been built by Vikings. Other scientists, of course, pooh-poohed this theory, and advanced some of their own, but the fact remains, that no one has ever satisfactorily explained the existence of these apparently typical Norse eider duck shelters on St. Helena Island.

All this I tried to explain to Akpaleeapik, in the vain hope of getting him interested enough to make some attempt to reach the island. The story fascinated him, but with typical Eskimo practicality he wanted to know if the kabloona "long, long ago" really lived here. No, I said, they lived in Greenland, but they may have come this far to see what the land was like. Then, he countered, what was the good of going to all the bother of building shelters for ducks unless you were sure you could come back each year to collect the down? And, anyway, no dice about even trying to reach the island now. It would be surrounded by a wide belt of open water. "Maybe you swim to island and live in little house, eh?" Akpaleeapik teased me, and with that he repacked the tea box, lashed it in its usual place on top of the load and we continued eastward.

We gave the towering pinnacle of Boat Point a wide berth, since for miles around it the ice had been thrown up into a chaos of contorted pressure ridges. Here Sverdrup had left his boat and sledged in late July into the still-frozen Viks Fiord. At Boat Point, too, he had found signs of previous human occupation. "The long rows of tent rings were unequivocal witnesses that we were not the first who had found a sheltered and comfortable camping ground here. In one place a fire had been made, and we found there a quantity of bones and train oil mixed together."

Sheltered the place had been, but also noisy. "What a turmoil was there! Thousands upon thousands of black guillemots were nesting in the steep mountainsides. . . . Out on the water they swarmed like ants in an anthill; the eiders and black guillemots kept things going ceaselessly with their shrilling and screaming high up in the treble, while the walruses grunted a steady-going bass, sometimes solo, sometimes in chorus."

Now the mountain stood silent and sombre against a deep blue sky, and around it the sea looked as if it had been quick-frozen in the midst of turmoil and tempest. Farther out on the sound, though, the ice was fairly smooth and after fifteen hours sledging we were back in Bear Bay. In the distance Skruis Point loomed up, where we had been more than a month ago.

Somehow it seemed much longer, as if we had sledged for many many months, over snow and land and ice, shooting each day our daily seal, setting camp with each item every day in its appointed place, breaking camp, loading the long sleds and travelling on, living constantly in the present, with little concern what tomorrow might bring, because one didn't know anyway and when it came one would cope with it. There was a comforting continuum of daily routine, and at the same time the constant change of travel. Since for weeks on end we did not see any other people, though travelling nearly continuously, this produced the strange sensation of being suspended in time and space, especially since day and night were now nearly equally bright and seemed to be a never-ending one, and space was predominantly white. I was surprised that, in all the Eskimo legends I had read, I had never come across a boreal version of the Flying Dutchman story, of an Eskimo doomed to sledge forever and ever through an endless frozen sea of ice and snow.

Now that the chances of meeting another bear were poor, Akpaleeapik was in a hurry to get home. A timid suggestion from me that we might sledge to Grise Fiord via Cape Sparbo, so I could photograph muskoxen there and look for Dr. Cook's house, met with no enthusiasm. The dogs were tired, Akpaleeapik said, and besides he had to pick up the foxes he had cached on the Ellesmere Island coast.

We slept less than usual, packed a bit faster than usual and headed north, seesawing across the drifts on Jones Sound. Halfway across the sound, a broad open lead barred the way and we sledged alongside it, to find a spot narrow enough to cross or an ice floe bridge. The lead, like a dark, jagged rent in an immense white cloth, meandered westward. It was full of life. Ringed seal popped up in the water and stared curiously at us with bulging eyes, but dived with a splash before Akpaleeapik could get his rifle. Ducks, already paired, paddled busily along making abrupt little bows to each other; and large flocks of black guillemots flew up where we passed, coral red feet trailing until they got well into the air.

At a place where the lead turned at a sharp angle a large floe had become wedged in it, forming a sort of bridge. Akpaleeapik

125

tried it and found it fairly safe provided not too much weight was put on it. He ran across, stepping lightly on the floe, and I followed, carrying the cameras.

"You stay here and call the dogs," Akpaleeapik said, and skipped back to the other side.

The dogs didn't like the idea of crossing and took immediate evasive action. After Akpaleeapik had thrashed them soundly, individually and collectively, while I was crooning enticingly from the far bank, they suddenly rushed forward, dashed across the flow and up onto firm ice on the other side—so fast, the sled passed across the floe before it had time to sink.

Akeeagok now lined up his sled and team. Akpaleeapik called the dogs, and I stood to one side to get pictures of the crossing. At the last instant, while most of Akeeagok's dogs dashed forward, a few balked. They were yanked pell-mell into the lead, but this drag was sufficient to stop the other dogs on the far side before the sled was across. It stopped on the floe, which slowly sank beneath its weight. Akeeagok and Seeglook jumped ahead and across as their sled settled into water. Akeeagok beat his dogs, while we hauled at the traces. The sled jerked forward, a third was already on firm ice, when the rear end slipped off the sinking floe. For an instant the heavily loaded sled teetered on the ice edge of the lead, partly in water and partly in the air. Then the dogs, alarmed by the fierce urgency in their master's voice, jumped into harness with all their might, we gave a concerted heave and the sled tilted forward and slid onto firm ice.

Four of Akeeagok's dogs were still in the water, trying to pull themselves up onto the ice, but their blunt claws kept slipping off and they howled dolefully. One of them was a spaniel-like little bitch, with floppy ears, an immensely thick, silky coat, and a sad face, the hair below her eyes always matted with tears. She had left Grise Fiord pregnant and had, in the course of our trip, expanded so alarmingly I suspected her of hatching two dozen pups. She usually padded along, literally *ventre à terre*, in a preoccupied and lachrymose manner, as if nursing some deep and secret sorrow. Because of her condition, and her tearful despoiled-virgin look, I had called her Gretchen, after the wronged heroine of Goethe's *Faust.* Now she was clinging to the ice rim, nearly waterlogged and more grief-stricken than ever. But each time Akeeagok reached for her, she slid back into the water and paddled about, whimpering pathetically, Finally he managed to get a hold of her torn trace and dragged Gretchen onto firm ice.

Altogether, it was a bad day for the dogs. It thawed a bit during the day but later froze again and, for the first time during the trip, Akpaleeapik and Akeeagok did not succeed in shooting a seal. We saw eighteen seals, and they stalked ten of them. But the frosted snow crackled sharply beneath their boots and betrayed them. Each time the stalked seal slid down into its hole before the hunter was within shooting range. It thawed again next day, and then they shot a couple of seals, but they did not feed them to the dogs until next night, when we camped again near the mighty mountain bastion of Cape Storm.

"Last sleep," Akpaleeapik said. This seemed incredible. We still had about eighty miles to go and some of our dogs were already limping badly. Alternate thawing and freezing had created sharp ice crystals and our teams left tracks dotted with blood from cut pads. But the men were anxious to get home. We slept during the warmth of the day and started as soon as the evening frost had hardened the snow surface, sledging fast past the magnificent, steep-cliffed mountains of southern Ellesmere Island.

Akeeagok, whose dogs were not as strong as Akpaleeapik's, gradually fell behind, and we stopped near South Cape to make tea and wait for him. I walked to the shore to photograph a strange hollow in the side of a cliff—created by a waterfall and looking somewhat like an immense scooped-out band shell. It seemed quite close, but it was not easy to get through the jumble of up-heaved ice floes near shore, since the spaces between them were now filled with little lakes of melt-water, the ice at their bottoms a strange vivid green. On shore, the first flowers were in bloom, tight little rosettes of purple saxifrage.

When I returned, I saw that Akeeagok had a new passenger. Gretchen had given birth on the trail, and despite here imposing girth, she had only produced three pups. Two had been killed instantly, but one Akeeagok had left her; and now, instead of pulling it, she was riding on the sled, all curled up to protect her pup from the cold wind, licking it tenderly and looking, for once, a little bit happy.

We sledged through the night and all next day. The snow became soft and sticky, the dogs strained in harness, tongues lolling, scooping up bogs of snow to quench their thirst, exhausted but willing. They, too, were eager to get home. After twenty-seven hours of steady sledging, we were back in Grise Fiord, nearly six weeks to the day since we had left it. When we were close to the settlement, the fagged dogs gathered their last strength and we arrived as we had left, caroming through the ice blocks near shore in a final exuberant gallop; and just as nearly everyone had been there to see us off, so everyone was there now to welcome us back.

CHAPTER TWELVE

Roger, well aware of priorities, invited me for a bath, dinner and drink, in that order, and we talked until the early hours of the next day.

"When are you starting your next trip?" he asked, jokingly.

"Well, as a matter of fact tomorrow, if possible," I said.

"Good heavens!" he exclaimed. "Don't you ever get enough? I should have thought six weeks sledging was plenty. Where do you want to go to now?"

I explained that I still had muskoxen on my mind and would like to hire someone with a fresh team of dogs to take me to Cape Sparbo on Devon Island.

Roger looked thoughtful. "We'll talk to Sam Willy about it tomorrow," he said. "Maybe he can take you by skidoo. That would be the fastest way."

Sam came to my cabin at lunch time. We had tea and talked. He had shot a wolf since we had been away. He had met the animal on fairly smooth ice far out on Jones Sound and had overtaken it easily enough with his skidoo. But each time he stopped and got his gun ready the wolf had already loped out of range. But finally the wolf tired and he had shot him.

After a while he came out with the main purpose of his visit. The ice between Grise Fiord and Cape Sparbo was rent by wide leads, he said. It would be nearly impossible to get across them with a skidoo and even if we did they could widen even more while we were on Devon Island, and we might not be able to come back. But with dogs and a lightly loaded sled, the trip might still be made.

"Do you know anyone who will take me?" I asked.

"Maybe Paulassee," Sam said. "I go and ask."

He returned in the afternoon with a meek little man, who sat a bit uneasily on the edge of his chair, while I brewed another pot of

Polar bear skins bleach on a clothes line in Grise Fiord while clouds hang low on the mountain sides

tea. He agreed to everything I asked, with a touching eagerness to please. Oh yes, he knew the "white man's house" at Cape Sparbo; he knew where the muskoxen were; he was sure we could be back within four days; he would take pots and pans, if I took food; and was there anything else I would like him to do? Well, yes, I said. Could we leave today? Of course, he assured me. We could go any time I wished, only, he added with a timid smile, it would be best to leave fairly late in the evening when travel conditions would be best.

What a change, I reflected, from my forceful and decisive friend Akpaleeapik. I had, of course, met Paulassee before and had even visited his home which he had nicely furnished and which his wife kept immaculate. But somehow the friendly, affable little man had left no impression. I remembered him mainly as the father of some of Grise Fiord's most charming children, round-faced little girls who had visited me at the cabin several times, giggling shyly when

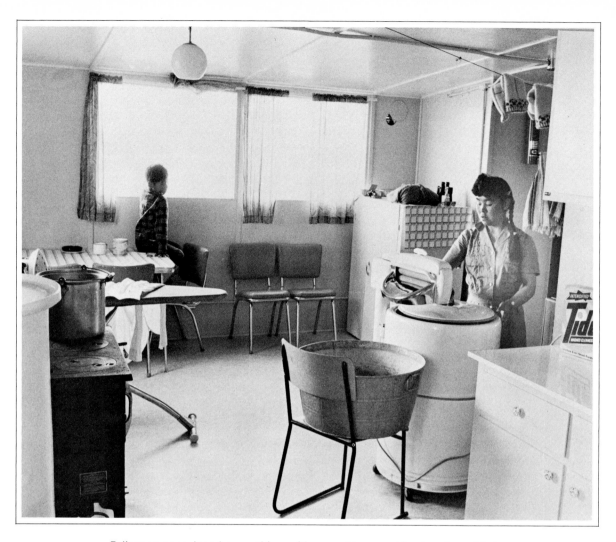

Eelisapee now does her washing with a washing machine in a large kitchen—ten years ago she lived in an igloo

I asked them something, watching everything I did with keen-eyed curiosity, and whose faces lit up into beautiful smiles when I offered them cookies. After an hour, they would all troop out, with a polite little "thank you," and I would look forward to their next visit. The cabin always seemed a bit brighter and happier when they were there. Now I watched their father with some apprehension. It was sixty miles across Jones Sound in a straight line from Grise Fiord to Cape Sparbo. With detours forced by leads and pressure ridges, we might have to travel eighty miles or more either way. It would have to be a fast, hard trip, and somehow Paulassee did not look the man for it.

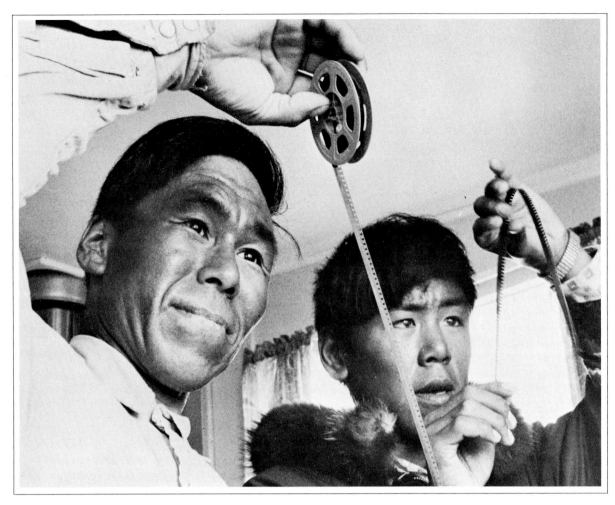

Elijah, Eelisapee's husband, looks at a film he has taken and which, after months in the south, has just arrived on one of the rare aircraft to visit Grise Fiord

My apprehensions grew in the late evening, when I saw his dogs. Six of them were fairly sturdy looking huskies, but four were demi-Labradors, half-brothers of Apapak! And these were only half the size of Apapak—small, nervous, yappy, fidgety dogs. Akpaleeapik had lent us his sled, much longer than Paulassee's and better suited for crossing leads. Paulassee loaded the sled, fussing and worrying, and asking repeatedly for my approval of the arrangements.

Paulassee had come to Grise Fiord from Port Harrison, while Akpaleeapik and Akeeagok were born in the Pond Inlet area of Baffin Island. Nothing could have been more different than their

132

ways of driving dog teams. Akpaleeapik directed his team with loud, guttural, authoritarian orders and, when these were not immediately obeyed, lit into the dogs with his thirty-foot rawhide whip. He commanded and expected instant obedience.

Paulassee's whip was a bit of thong nailed to a stick, so short it did not even reach the dog nearest the sled. His commands, high-pitched, bird-like chirps, seemed to lack even the pretense of authority, and the dogs blithely ignored them. Akpaleeapik's dogs respected their stern master and also feared him; they'd cringe when he was angry. Paulassee's dogs had no respect at all for their little master, but they seemed to be genuinely fond of him and, whenever we stopped, they'd all come trooping back to say "hallo," and got their traces tangled up something awful.

Now we started across Jones Sound and the dogs ran wherever it pleased them paying no attention to Paulassee's entreating chirrups. Whenever they got too far off course, he hopped off the sled and sprinted in the right direction, chirping like a mother sparrow, the dogs veered, he shooed them on, and hopped back on the sled as it passed.

Unless the ice was very bad, Akpaleeapik rarely left the sled. To steer such a long, low and heavy sled is extremely hard work. On level ice or snow, the front of the sled can only slowly be eased around by a man running beside it and pressing against it with all his force. When the sled crosses a ridge, its course can be abruptly changed by a push or pull at the precise instant when it teeters on the top of the ridge. Akpaleeapik seldom bothered. His dogs were strong and he made them do the work of changing course as the terrain required.

Paulassee rarely sat still on his sled for two minutes in a row. He hopped off, guided it around an obstacle or over a ridge and hopped on again, with amazing agility, making it as easy on his dogs as possible and keeping them in this way, too, on a fairly straight course.

We sledged for six hours, long stretches of bad pressure ice alternating with reasonably level areas. It was cold, humid and windy, and the chill crept through my clothes, although I did run a great deal beside the sled. For the last hour or two, I kept hoping Paulassee would stop for tea. But on he went, pulling the heavy sled this way and that, hopping off and on like a superactive chirpy little cricket.

Suddenly he turned to me and asked with a timid smile: "Is it all right to stop for tea?"

133

I was flabbergasted and quite conscience-stricken. Akpaleeapik, quite rightly, since he was in command of the trip, had never asked me anything. When he felt like having tea, we had tea. He decided when we travelled and where we travelled, and when and where we camped. To me he showed great kindness and consideration and, with a natural tact, put his orders in the form of requests or suggestions. But there was never any question but that he was in charge, and naturally all the decisions of the trip were his. I was so used to this arrangement, it had never occurred to me that Paulassee might expect me to decide when to stop for tea.

Now I tried to impress upon him that, of course, he could stop any time he pleased and travel any way he thought right; that all I wanted was to reach Cape Sparbo, see muskoxen and Dr. Cook's house, but that as far as the rest of the trip was concerned he was in charge. He smiled gently and nodded, but I realized he had not understood me. Paulassee did not know a word of English and, coming from Port Harrison, spoke an Eskimo dialect I found extremely hard to understand, nor could he grasp the words I had so laboriously learned from Eskimos of other regions. Our mutually intelligible vocabulary consisted of about twenty words, and in his eagerness to please me, Paulassee smilingly agreed with everything I said, regardless of whether he understood me or not.

The Eskimos of Siberia, Alaska, the Canadian Arctic, Labrador and Greenland all speak the same language, but with strong regional dialects. In Grise Fiord, where Eskimos from two very distinct dialect areas live in one settlement, they have become accustomed to each other's way of speaking. They understand each other well, and the children speak a mixture of both dialects. But Baffin Island Eskimos listening to broadcasts in Eskimo from Greenland, find them fairly hard to follow.

As we travelled on, I began to realize that I had seriously underestimated the strength and stamina of both Paulassee and his dogs. The dogs kept running at a steady trot, hour after hour, and Paulassee never seemed to tire from pushing that heavy sled around. We came to two wide leads, and were both times fortunate to find ice bridges across without having to make long detours. After fourteen hours we reached Cape Hardy on Devon Island, sledged around it and made camp on a raised beach above a sheltered little bay.

"Where is the kabloona's igloo?" I asked Paulassee.

He looked blank, then pulled out a map and pointed to a neat, pencilled x made near Cape Sparbo, Cape Hardy's sister cape.

"Akpaleeapik say house here," he said.

"And where are the muskoxen?" I asked, with a sinking feeling. Sure enough, he pointed to another little x on the map.

"Sam Willy say oomingmak here," he explained, with an ingenuous little smile.

I realized now that he didn't have a clue. He merely had said "yes" to everything in Grise Fiord to please me, and had then gone and asked some of the other men who really were familiar with the Cape Sparbo area. To look for something in the Arctic whose exact location you do not know, I remembered from bitter experience, is a well-nigh hopeless task, unless you have lots of time. My happy vision of being led straight to Dr. Cook's house and to some herds of muskoxen, was now replaced by the stark probability that we would not be able to find either. I was tired and angry, and for one horrible moment I was on the verge of shouting: "But you told me you yourself knew!" But then I saw Paulassee's kind, eager face, and felt like a cad.

"Never mind," I said. "We'll have to look. Get me the pot and I'll make breakfast."

"What pot?" Paulassee asked.

"Didn't you bring pots and a pan?"

"No. No pot. Maybe this?" he hopefully held up the tea kettle.

I made porridge in the kettle, and since Paulassee had also omitted to bring any sort of eating utensils, we ate it alternately with the spoon I had fortunately taken along. Replete and mollified, I suggested we go and look for Dr. Cook's house, and we started the long walk around Cape Hardy.

Cape Hardy, and Cape Sparbo a couple of miles farther west along the north Devon Island coast, jut far out into Jones Sound. From a distance the two one-thousand-foot promontories look like islands. Beyond this sombre rock bulwark, stretches a great plain of rolling meadows and lakes, intersected by high gravel ridges, about fifteen miles wide and five miles deep, ending abruptly at the inland cliffs that rise steeply to a fifteen-hundred-foot-high plateau above.

Dr. Frederick A. Cook may or may not have been the first man to reach the North Pole. Most authorities today agree that he wasn't anywhere near it. Unfortunately this rather deplorable lack of verisimilitude, and all the vicious mudslinging that went on between him and Peary, the man who presumably did reach the pole, and between Cook's partisans and Peary's partisans, has obscured the fact that Dr. Cook made one of the most amazing trips in the history of arctic exploration.

He had already taken part in several Arctic and Antarctic expeditions. In 1907, he accompanied a wealthy American sportsman, J. R. Bradley, on a hunting trip to the Arctic. They ended up among the Polar Eskimos at Annoatok in northwestern Greenland. There Cook decided to have a crack at the Pole. He left with a group of Eskimos in February, 1908, crossed Ellesmere Island, and sledged to the north tip of Axel Heiberg Island. There he dismissed all the Eskimos, except two young men, Etukishook and Ahwelah, and pushed on with two sleds, twenty-six dogs, and rations that can only be described as meagre. He later claimed to have travelled from there to the pole and back.

Summer breakup caught him near Devon Island. He tried to reach Greenland in a small canvas boat, was caught and mauled by storms and drifting ice, and finally ended up at Cape Sparbo, half starved and in desperate straits. "Our dogs were gone. Our ammunition, except for four cartridges which I had secreted for use in a last emergency, was gone. Our equipment consisted of a half sledge (the other half had been cut up to make harpoon shafts), a canvas boat (torn), a torn silk tent, a few camp kettles, tin plates, knives and matches. Our clothing was splitting to shreds."[1] They had no sleeping bags, no winter clothing, no weapons and no food. And the arctic winter was a month away.

At Cape Sparbo they discovered a fairly roomy den which, centuries before, had already served Eskimos as shelter. They made harpoons and lances, killed seals, made rope from the seal skins and snared and killed muskoxen. When winter came, they had ample meat and bulky fur clothes. Then began the long hibernation in their stone den, illuminated only by the weak, flickering light of stone lamps in which they burnt muskox tallow. Temperatures dropped to fifty and sixty degrees below zero, and polar bears prowled hungrily around their cave, trying to get at their stock of frozen meat and fat.

After spending more than one hundred days and nights in this icy, tomb-like hole, they set out to walk to Greenland, pulling all their possessions on the remnants of their sled. They reached Annoatok, after weeks of harrowing hardships, at the end of March 1909. In the subsequent hullabaloo between Cook and Peary about who had reached the pole first, if at all, Cook's amazing feat of endurance and ingenuity was all but forgotten. Much, if not most of the credit for his survival must go to his two Eskimo companions, but there is no doubt that all three men showed an amazing resourcefulness at Cape Sparbo. The Eskimos later substantiated this portion of Cook's narrative, at least in its broad outlines, because in his book he felt

[1]In Dr. Frederick A. Cook, *My Attainment of the Pole* (New York and London: Mitchell and Kennedy, 1912).

136

obliged to embellish an already amazing tale with such odd inventions as the visit of "blue rats" who, he says, came crawling in the dead of winter into his subterranean lair to hibernate there. But making all due allowance for Cook's vivid imagination (and still more vivid prose), his was still one of the great polar trips and I was anxious to see the hole in which he and his two companions had spent the winter.

Paulassee, who had sensed that I was annoyed because he did not know the exact location of the house, was keen to make amends. He walked ahead at a brisk pace and found half a dozen "houses," all remains of former Eskimo dwellings. Each time he would look at me with eager, hopeful eyes and ask: "This house okay?" At the sixth house which, like the others, did not at all correspond to Dr. Cook's description of his den, I just didn't have the heart to say again, "No, this isn't it." So I assured Paulassee this was the very house I was seeking and he looked so pleased it made me feel good.

On the way back to camp, Paulassee spotted a seal not very far from the jumble of tidal ice ridges surrounding the cape. He walked stealthily closer, keeping out of sight behind blocks of ice. From the last sheltering block it was still too far for a sure shot at such a small target as a seal's head. He had no hunting screen along, so he had recourse to another Eskimo method of hunting seal—pretending to be a seal himself. He waited until the seal had finished its thorough examination of the surrounding area and, satisfied that all was safe, had gone to sleep again.

Paulassee emerged from his shelter, ran fast for twenty yards or so, then lay down on the ice and slithered towards the seal on his belly and elbows, pushing himself forward with his feet. When the seal awoke, Paulassee lay motionless. The seal saw him and stared intently. Paulassee rolled to one side, and made a flipper-like scratching motion in superb imitation of seal movements. Seals are wary but fairly shortsighted, and what this seal thought it saw was something that looked like another seal and behaved like one. Reassured the seal went back to sleep, and Paulassee immediately began to creep forward again. Each time the seal woke up, he stopped and, if the seal appeared suspicious, made some typical seal-like movement. In fifteen minutes he had crawled to within good range and shot the seal through the head.

We walked back to camp and, while I cooked a pot of stew, Paulassee harnessed some of the dogs and fetched the seal. The stew tasted of tea and the tea afterwards tasted of stew, but we were far too famished to quibble.

137

After a few hours' sleep, we sledged from Cape Hardy to Cape Sparbo and set up camp on a level stretch of raw-sienna coloured, disintegrated rock, obviously a camping place of hunters since time immemorial. Tent rings were everywhere, and cairns and large stone caches. We walked inland and as we came over a ridge, saw nine muskoxen grazing peacefully on a bare patch of ground ahead of us. We ducked before they saw us.

"Go get dog," I told Paulassee. "Dog stop oomingmak."

He trotted off and reappeared shortly, dragging an extremely reluctant husky along on a rope, a shaggy yellow-brown creature, with slanted wolf-like eyes of a most peculiar faded blue colour. As soon as we appeared above the ridge, the muskoxen became uneasy, milled about in apparent indecision and, suddenly making up their minds, wheeled about and took off at a gallop.

"Let go dog!" I called to Paulassee, as we ran after them.

The dog had seen the muskoxen and, since they ran away, pursued them eagerly. As he came close to the fleeing animals, they wheeled again and clustered together into their hedgehog formation, with admirable swiftness and precision. The dog, still eager, ran up to them. The muskoxen snorted and pawed the ground, and one of them charged with a speed that seemed incredible for such a clumsy looking animal. The dog leapt back just in time to evade a slash from the hooked horns, and came trotting back towards us in a thoroughly frightened and dejected manner.

The muskoxen were still very excited and belligerent, so we sat down and had a smoke, to give them time to relax a bit. Paulassee, as always, carried his gun.

"Would you shoot a muskox if he attacked me?" I asked, half joking.

Paulassee looked horrified. "Oh no!" he exclaimed. "I shoot oomingmak—government do—*so*" and he drew an expressive finger across his throat. He obviously carried a very vivid picture of the law's retributive wrath in his mind. In Canada, muskoxen are fully protected and it does no good to plead self-defence. This is right, because muskoxen, if left alone, are perfectly harmless, and anyone who goes so close as to get himself hooked has no one to blame but himself.

The light was miserable, so hazy and blue I felt certain that not even my filters would be able to restore a reasonable colour balance. In addition, it started to snow. I set up the camera on a tripod, covered it with a plastic bag, and we settled down to wait until the weather improved a bit. The muskoxen slowly resigned themselves to this unpleasant company. In order not to annoy them, we had tied up the dog out of sight behind a big boulder.

Paulassee whiled away the time by telling me, with very explicit gestures, the horrid story of an encounter between dogs and muskoxen. A Grise Fiord man had gone to a valley to hunt hares. He drove over a ridge and right into a herd of muskoxen. He couldn't stop his dogs who raced towards the muskoxen. He threw himself off the sled and the dogs, still harnessed and tied to the sled, dashed up to the muskoxen, already drawn up in battle formation. A great bull charged, skewered one of the dogs, threw him up with a jerk that half eviscerated him and then trampled the poor beast. The other dogs tried to get away from the enraged bull, but they got tangled up in their traces and two more were gored to death before the rest escaped.

Our muskoxen now looked as placid as contented cows. Some had lain down, and were chewing their cud in a bored, methodical manner. If I moved very slowly, they would let me come to within fifteen feet, without getting unduly annoyed. The lead bull snorted and rubbed his head against a rock, but he did so in a fairly mild, perfunctory manner, and not in that wild-eyed "you-come-one-step-closer-and-I-hook-you" attitude of a really provoked bull.

The light improved. I photographed the muskoxen from every angle I could think of, while they watched my posturings with vague interest. Our tête-à-tête had now lasted three hours, and they seemed quite resigned to my importunate presence.

Since these might well be the only muskoxen we would see, I wanted a few pictures with a bit more action. All I had, up to now, were of a nice group of muskoxen looking placid, bored and a trifle blasé. I knew what would perk them up.

"Paulassee, can you turn the dog loose?" I asked.

The dog was sound asleep behind his rock and in no mood to do battle with sharp-horned muskoxen. He listened to Paulassee's exhortations without enthusiasm, took another look at the musk-oxen, and retired behind his rock again to resume his interrupted sleep.

"Bring him here," I said, without thinking.

And good little Paulassee, who knew perfectly well that my request was asinine and dangerous, came up dragging the unwilling dog behind him. We immediately got plenty of action. The bull charged, I dashed one way, Paulassee hopped squirrel-quick behind a boulder, and the dog, suddenly wide awake, streaked off towards camp. Fortunately the bull's fury was mainly directed against the dog and, having put him to rout, he returned majestically to his herd, his dark hair skirt swaying with every step.

Rather shaken I collected my camera gear and we returned to camp. After lunch, we began to walk all round Cape Sparbo. We found some fairly large, conical stone structures, each with an entrance at the side. Paulassee said such houses had, in former days, served as ambushes for hunters. We found many stone fox traps and, on the west side of Cape Sparbo, the remains of several Eskimo houses, with a profusion of whale bones and caribou bones strewn about. Large clusters of purple saxifrage bloomed on the gravel ridges. In the evening we came across a herd of seven muskoxen. The wind was bad, and they took off in a hurry. We did not have the dog along to stop them.

In a grassy depression between gravel ridges, we discovered a second herd with a magnificent bull, nearly black and with a superb sweep of horns, polished and glowing against his dark fur in that soft yellow of very old ivory. The herd grouped into defensive position, but I had only just set up my tripod and taken some pictures, with the snow-covered mountains of Devon Island forming a superb background, when some of the animals started to shift position. Then all began to mill and jostle, and suddenly they took off, galloping in tight formation towards the mountains in the distance. Later we saw them walk single-file on a high gravel ridge, dark, massive silhouettes against a grim, grey, wintry sky.

We went to bed early and I was up again at 1 A.M. Sleepy, and still in my underwear, I went for a little walk. My kamiks had been wet in the evening. Now their soles were frozen and icy. I slipped on a rock and fell full length, my back hitting the sharp edge of another boulder. I rolled off and lay on the ground, contorted by such pain I thought I must have damaged my spine. After a while I managed to get up and walk back to the tent. We had breakfast and I could feel my body stiffen. If we stayed there much longer, I realized, I would not be able to move. Paulassee, fortunately, had not noticed anything and was his usual cheerful, chipper self.

We walked across the great plain towards the inland mountains, Paulassee with the husky in tow. The heavy clouds began to shift and rift, the sun broke through, it became quite warm and soon the plain was covered with a lacework of murmuring rills and glistening pools. There were muskox tracks everywhere. Those we thought to be of "our" herd—the large group we had seen the previous evening—led straight towards a narrow, boulder-strewn valley that rose steeply to the inland plateau.

At the entrance to the valley, we found the half-eaten carcass of a muskox. Wolves, Paulassee thought, had feasted on it. We sat down on some boulders and ate bread Paulassee's wife had baked for us. It was not the usual pancake-shaped bannock, but a long, rope-like coil of dough that had been boiled in oil, in the manner of doughnuts. A specialty of the Eskimos of the Port Harrison area, Paulassee proudly explained. "You like?" he asked anxiously, and when I assured him it was marvellous, he smiled with pleasure.

I had taken a couple of boxes of raisins along. I broke one in half, gave Paulassee his share and greedily ate mine with the bread. He ate a few, wrapped the rest carefully in a handkerchief and put them into his satchel.

"Eat," I urged him. "I got another box."

He wrinkled his nose to "no," and smiled: "I take home for children," he said. He always thought of everyone else before himself.

It took us several hours to reach the plateau. I marvelled how the muskoxen had marched up steep snow slopes and wended their way through chaotic masses of boulders. On the plateau, there was no sign of them. From a high mountain we had a magnificent view of the north shore of Devon Island, but no muskoxen were to be seen anywhere. The sun had softened the snow surface and increasingly often we broke through and floundered in hip-deep, sticky snow. Paulassee, who must have been utterly fed up with all this useless toil, marched on, uncomplaining and cheerful.

After twelve hours, wet and exhausted, I gave up. These muskoxen had travelled fast and far. We glissaded down the steeper snow slopes, saw a couple of ptarmigan who were so tame I could walk to within a few feet of them, and were back on the plain in a couple of hours. We sat down and smoked; then Paulassee, always alert, suddenly said: "Oomingmak!" The herd we were seeking was grazing a couple of miles away near the foot of the cliffs. The muskoxen must have been in a gully when we first crossed the plain and we had wasted fourteen hours working our way through wet snow in pursuit of quite another herd. As a pair of trackers, we certainly were a failure.

We grabbed our bags and walked fast towards the muskoxen. The sun was still high and the light perfect. I ran ahead, while Paulassee dragged the unwilling dog along, turned around some boulders that had fallen from the cliff, and nearly bumped into a great solitary muskox bull. The surprise was mutual. The bull had been lying behind a boulder, dreamily chewing his cud, when I

Near the cliffs of Devon Island Paulassee found a dead muskox, partly eaten by wolves

suddenly burst in on him and stopped, sharply, three feet away. He jumped up with a snort and I hopped back behind the boulders with alacrity. When Paulassee arrived, I took a careful peek around the rock. The bull was galloping full tilt towards the herd, and another solitary bull, who must have been amongst the boulders, joined him.

We raced after them, the husky excited by the sight of fleeing animals, pulling Paulassee forward, with all the impetuousness of a large dog taking a six-year-old child for a walk. The two bulls reached the herd and all the animals lined up, not in the usual tight

142

As we walked down from the Devon Island mountains a ptarmigan flew up and landed on a nearby rock, more curious than afraid

formation, but abreast in one long line. When we got to within thirty yards, we stopped among some small rocks. I unpacked all the camera gear and finished the roll of film in each camera. I was about to kneel down to change films, when the herd began its typical wheeling shuffle. Any moment now, they would run.

"Let the dog loose!" I called to Paulassee.

The husky ran towards the herd, the animals started to flee, the dog was suddenly amongst them and the next instant Paulassee dashed forward. The dog had caught a calf! The herd, still milling, suddenly scattered. Paulassee reached the dog and kicked it away from the little calf, and in the next moment there was utter confusion.

The herd raced past Paulassee, who ducked behind a boulder, and galloped towards me in wild-eyed panic. The calf trotted after them, could not keep up and disappeared behind some rocks. The nineteen adult muskoxen were only fifteen yards away and I didn't know what to do: run and get my scattered camera equipment trampled, or make a stand. I crouched down and, at the last moment, jumped up, flung my arms wide and yelled at the top of my voice. The herd parted and dashed past within a couple of yards on either side of me.

The dog was after the muskoxen again and brought them to a stop some fifty yards further on. Only the two solitary bulls who had joined the herd continued in their flight, heading for the cliffs. The other muskoxen lined up in a defensive circle, making lightning-quick sorties when the dog came close. Paulassee managed to catch the dog again and sat down on a rock at a respectful distance from the herd.

They were beautiful and impressive animals, standing there shoulder to shoulder and glowering at me. The bull and the largest cows had taken up key positions facing their enemies. The young animals were kept in the center. Once a curious yearling started forward, and was immediately butted back into line by one of the older animals.

My hands were shaking so badly, I could not change film; so I sat and smoked to let myself and the muskoxen calm down. This was a very different group from the one I had photographed the previous day. As soon as I came to within forty feet, the great bull, his curved horns gleaming dull yellow in the sun, took a couple of slow, regal steps forward, pawed the ground and snorted loudly. He, it seemed, would stand for no nonsense.

The two solitary bulls had climbed through a maze of enormous boulders at the base of the cliff. Now they started to walk obliquely upward on a steep field of scree and snow, with the sure-footed skill of mountain goats. I watched their stately progress with fascination and fear, feeling responsible for their flight and worried lest they fall and hurt themselves. Dislodged stones clattered down the mountain, but the two bulls continued upwards until they had reached a shelf near the foot of the sheer cliff. There they turned around, their backs to the rock, their well-armed heads facing outward. To any enemy, except a man with a gun, theirs was an impregnable position. I climbed after them to take pictures. They must have felt absolutely secure on their rock shelf, since they dispensed even with the normal motions of excitation and anger. They did not paw, snort, or rub their heads against rocks or their

144

forelegs. They stood stolid, and stared down at me with quiet composure.

Then I went to look for the little calf, and found it sound asleep behind a boulder. It had dark, curly hair, a light grey muzzle, white stockings, and a cream-coloured saddle. In all, it was a miniature edition of its parents. The only thing it lacked was the long mantle of guard hairs. I examined it carefully and found that, thanks to its heavy fur, the dog had not injured it. When I touched it, the calf woke up, rose on wobbly legs and tried to butt me. It was an adorable, defiant and scared little creature, and I felt very guilty about its predicament. I picked it up. The calf struggled furiously at first, and bleated loudly, like a lonely lamb. Finding it could not escape, it resigned itself and lay quietly in my arms, as I walked slowly with it towards the herd. At fifty feet I put the calf down, pointed it in the right direction and gave it a little push. But it just stood there, looking pathetically forlorn. I picked it up again and slowly carried it closer to the herd, uncomfortably aware that ahead of me was a bereft muskox mother, and having no idea what her reaction might be.

The herd had calmed down a great deal and the muskoxen were watching my approach without showing too much anger. Every time they began to snort and paw, I stopped, talking softly to the calf, hoping to keep it quiet. But every once in a while it would let out one of those shrill, plaintive bleats, setting all my taut nerves ajangle. Paulassee, perched on his rock, watched the performance with worried fascination. At twenty feet, one of the muskoxen pushed himself out of the defensive ring and came a few steps forward. I put the calf down and walked slowly backwards, as one retreats from royalty.

I waved to Paulassee to go, picked up my bags and, making a wide circle around the herd, joined him a mile further on. We sat down on a ridge and watched the herd. They still stood as we had left them, but after a while they slowly moved, in a tight group, towards the calf. Keeping in sight as much as possible, to reassure the animals that we were actually departing, we walked back to the camp and reached it, hungry and tired, in the late evening.

We had an immense meal, hitched the dogs to the sled and set off for Grise Fiord. I felt exhausted from our twenty-hour walk, but Paulassee, who looked so small and frail, showed no sign of strain. He sat on the front of the sled, hopped off to steer it and on again when it was on course, directing his dogs with chipper chirps which they continued to ignore.

The little muskox calf, covered in thick curly wool, stands still a bit wobbly on its short legs

Two ivory gulls flew over the ice and accompanied us for many miles with shrill tern-like cries. This high arctic species is one of the smallest and certainly one of the most beautiful members of the gull family: immaculately white, with short dark beak and tiny black feet, and long, slender wings. In flight, ivory gulls are a vision of loveliness, so pure and white and elegant, they seem like the embodiment of some celestial being. It therefore came as a shock to realize that their main motive for following us, was to eat the dogs' excrement.

The calf near the herd—after we left, the herd slowly moved away, taking with them the calf they had earlier abandoned

Halfway across Jones Sound, we came to a wide lead and sledged for hours alongside it without finding an ice bridge. Finally we came to a place, where the lead curved around a small iceberg.

Paulassee got his harpoon shaft out and a hatchet, we broke pieces of ice from the berg, threw them into the open water and shoveled lots of snow on top; added more ice and more snow and after a few hours' hard work we had a reasonably good bridge across the lead. The dogs, as usual, would have none of it and, unlike Akpaleeapik, Paulassee would not beat his dogs into submission. So we pushed the sled across, ran across it ourselves and jumped to the other side and then pulled the dogs after us by their traces.

We sledged on for a while and then stopped for tea. Paulassee seemed preoccupied and worried. After several starts, followed by awkward silences, he summoned his courage and put it all into one word: "Okay?" I knew what he meant. After sledging, running, climbing and walking, with little sleep and rest, for four nights and three days, Paulassee was still worried whether I was satisfied with him. I was deeply touched by his concern and wanted to thank him properly, but it is extremely difficult to be effusive with a vocabulary of twenty words. The best I could do was to shake his hand and say: "Yes, Paulassee, very, very okay!" His brown, friendly face became suffused with one of his kind, cheerful smiles, and we sledged on, tired but happy, and reached Grise Fiord at noon next day.

The last three days I spent in Grise Fiord were crowded with meetings. All the men were now back from their spring hunts and it was the time for communal meetings. Grise Fiord's housing authority met at Roger's house, pored over maps and blueprints to determine the best locations for the last of the modern houses due on the government icebreaker that summer. The Reverend Howard Bracewell from Pond Inlet had arrived for the annual mission, and all members of the community met daily for services and prayer. Some Eskimos had donated their old houses, and all helped to tear them apart and to build, with this material, a small church. The Co-op members met, elected a new board of directors and they, in turn, elected Akpaleeapik as their president. The Community Council held its annual election, and Akpaleeapik was chosen as secretary. I attended and photographed the meetings, and although

Facing page:

Akeeagok prays during the service held by the missionary who comes once a year, if possible, from Pond Inlet, Baffin Island

148

Nearly all adults of Grise Fiord attend the community council meeting held in the school

I could only get the gist of the discussions, I was amazed at the astuteness with which the Eskimos tackled a wide range of local problems.

The third evening, the radio had a message for me. A plane was coming to Grise Fiord with mail and Sam Willy's wife, who had been to the hospital in Frobisher Bay to have her baby.

The next day looked grim. There was sun above Devon Island and, in the distance, we could see its icefields glitter; but on our side of Jones Sound, fog hung low on the mountains. At noon we heard the plane. It circled a couple of times, emerged suddenly from the grey murk and landed on the ice.

The pilot was in a rush to leave. "The fog is spreading," he said. I shook hands all around, climbed into the plane and minutes later we rose steeply above the ice of Jones Sound. The fog thinned, grew whiter and lighter; suddenly we were out of it and flew in glorious sunshine high above Jones Sound, the mountains of Devon Island and the wide expanse of Wellington Channel.

Two months ago I had stared in fascination at this immense land of black and white, so cold, so rugged and remote, and, apparently, without life. How, I had wondered, could anyone possibly exist here? Since then, Akpaleeapik, and Akeeagok, and Paulassee had given me the answer.